The H.A.V.E Effect

The H.A.V.E Effect

Why Your Faith Works on Sunday and Fades by Monday

James E. Nance II

THE H.A.V.E. EFFECT

Why Your Faith Works on Sunday and Fades by Monday

Intentionally Blank

"Now may the God of peace himself sanctify you completely, and may your whole spirit and soul and body be kept blameless." — 1 Thessalonians 5:23

Contents

Acknowledgments

To My Family

Katalina, my beloved wife and ministry partner — thank you for believing in this message before it was finished, and for walking through every hard season with me while I wrote it. Your partnership in this work has taught me more about what these principles look like in real life than any study ever could. Your wisdom, patience, and willingness to live these things alongside me have given this book its authenticity. None of this exists without you.

To my son Tre and my daughter Zoe — thank you for being exactly who you are, and for inspiring me to leave something worth inheriting. Watching you grow has given me a clarity of purpose I could not have manufactured on my own. I pray this book becomes part of what you carry forward — not just words, but a framework for the life God designed you for.

To my mother, Versia — thank you for the conversation that helped me push through to finish. When you reminded me that the Lord had given me something worth sharing, it was the fuel I needed. Your belief in what God placed in me has been a steady source of strength.

To my dad, James — thank you for planting the seed early, for keeping me in church, for grounding me in the Word. The biblical foundation you gave me in childhood became the soil where everything in this book eventually took root.

To the Sunday/Monday Gap Community

To every person who has trusted me to coach them, who completed an assessment, who showed up to a call and told the truth about where they were — thank you. Your willingness to be honest about the gap and your commitment to addressing it have made this book real. You are not illustrations. You are the proof.

To those who engaged with early versions of this material and gave feedback that sharpened every chapter — your honesty about what landed and what didn't make this a better resource for everyone who will read it.

To Beta Readers and Early Supporters

To everyone who read early drafts and offered honest feedback — this book is better because of you. To those who shared their own stories and allowed them to shape the composite portraits in these chapters — thank you for your courage. Your testimony will free people you will never meet.

To My Prayer Warriors

To everyone who is committed to praying for this project — I believe your intercession helped this book exist. I am convinced your continued prayer will multiply its reach in ways neither of us can anticipate.

To Future Multipliers

To the coaches, small group leaders, pastors, and teachers who will take this material and carry it further than I can alone — thank you in advance. I may not know your name yet, but I am grateful for your willingness to multiply what God started here.

A Word of Worship

Most importantly, I acknowledge and thank my Lord and Savior, who pulled me out of the gap I was living in and showed me that disorder is not a life sentence. Any truth in these pages comes from Him. Any error is my own. My prayer is that He uses these words to set people free and bring glory to His name.

The vision to help people close the gap between Sunday and Monday — to see believers living aligned, whole, and fruitful from one day to the next — comes from Him. The calling is His assignment. The book is His vessel.

To Him be the glory. May the H.A.V.E. Effect multiply His kingdom until every tribe, tongue, and nation knows the abundant life He offers.

Introduction

Two years ago, I was sitting in my car outside a grocery store, staring at a bank notification on my phone that our account was overdrawn — again.

My wife, Katalina, was inside shopping with a carefully calculated list, trying to stretch our limited budget to feed our family. I sat in the parking lot and did what I had been doing for months: wrestling. With failure. With inadequacy. With the growing, quiet suspicion that something in my life was fundamentally not working.

And here is what made it harder to name. I was a coach. I was helping people discover their purpose to live in alignment with God's design for their lives. I was coaching men through the gap between who they believed they were and how they were living. And then I sat in parking lots, overdrawn, wondering if I had missed something that everyone else seemed to have found.

The irony was not lost on me. I was living in the gap, trying to help other people close what I was living in.

That morning, I had scrolled through social media and seen ministry leaders celebrating new buildings, successful conferences, and milestones that felt impossibly far from where we were. The comparison was not motivating. It was a weight. Here I was, faithfully trying to serve, and the life I was describing from the outside was not the life I was experiencing on the inside. Sunday's clarity was real. Monday's reality was something else entirely.

The gap between Sunday and Monday is not a spiritual problem. It is a structural one.

That afternoon in the parking lot, something shifted.

Not the bank balance. Not the circumstances. But something in the interior. As I sat there cycling through the familiar thoughts — maybe I'm not cut out for this, maybe I should get a regular job, maybe God's plan isn't going to happen for me — I heard something different. Not audible. But unmistakable. A whisper from the Holy Spirit that landed with more weight than anything the noise had been saying:

"You already have what you need."

I sat with that for a long time.

What did I already have? A wife who believed in the calling. A Bible worn from years of study. A community of people I was genuinely serving. And access to the same God who had given Moses a staff, David five stones, a widow a jar of oil, and a boy five loaves and two fish. Every one of those stories followed the same pattern: the provision was already present. The problem was not absence. It was misalignment. The people in those stories were not lacking what they needed. They were not yet positioned to see what they already had access to.

XII

That whisper sent me into Scripture with different eyes. And what I found there changed everything about how I understood the problem I had been trying to solve — in my own life and in the lives of everyone I was coaching.

The Problem Beneath the Problem

Most believers are not struggling because they lack faith.

They are struggling because their lives are structurally misaligned with their beliefs.

That distinction took me years to understand, and it is the sentence this entire book is built on. Because if the problem is a lack of faith, the solution is more faith. More prayers. More commitment. More intensity. And most sincere believers have tried all those things and found that the clarity they produce fades faster than the week it arrives.

But if the problem is structural — if the interior architecture of a person's life has not been rebuilt to hold what their faith keeps offering — then trying harder at spiritual practices is like putting better fuel into an engine that is misaligned. The effort is real. Sincerity is genuine. But the structure underneath cannot sustain what the effort is trying to produce.

This is what I have been living. And when I finally had language for it, I understood why every recommitment had produced the same cycle: clarity on Sunday, erosion by Wednesday, distance by Friday, and the quiet discouragement of a person who had tried enough times to start wondering if the problem was permanent.

It is not permanent. But it is structural. And structural problems require structural solutions.

The book you are holding is my attempt to give that structure a name, a diagnosis, and a direction.

The Sunday/Monday Gap

I call it the Sunday/Monday Gap.

It is the distance between who you are in the designated spiritual moments of your life and who you are in the ordinary hours that follow. The version of yourself that shows up in worship and the version that shows up at work on Monday morning. The conviction that arrives with genuine force and the reality that arrives by Thursday, when that same conviction has quietly retreated, and you are not entirely sure when it left.

The gap is not evidence of hypocrisy. It is not proof of weak faith or insufficient commitment. It is the predictable experience of a human being whose interior has not yet been rebuilt to hold what the spirit keeps receiving.

The human being was designed with a specific interior order: spirit governing, soul following, body expressing. In that sequence, what the spirit receives from God flows through the soul and into the practical, daily decisions of an embodied life. Faith does not just live in Sunday's worship. It structures Monday's choices. It governs Tuesday's responses. It holds through Friday's pressures. The gap between Sunday and Monday closes not because you try harder to carry Sunday into Monday, but because the interior architecture has been rebuilt so that there is no longer a division between the two.

That is the life this book points toward.

Not a life without difficulty. A life whose governing center holds through difficulty. Not a life of perpetual spiritual elevation. A life in which faith has moved from the designated spiritual moments into the structure of the ordinary days, so that the person who shows up on Sunday and the person who shows up on Monday are the same, governed by the same interior, drawing from the same source.

A life that holds together is the result of alignment, not effort.

The H.A.V.E. Effect

As I went deeper into Scripture, tracing the pattern of restoration through the biblical narrative, four things kept emerging as the marks of a life that had genuinely closed the gap. Four qualities that characterized the person in whom faith and ordinary life had stopped dividing against each other and had begun to move together.

I call them the H.A.V.E. Effect.

Hope. Abundance. Virtue. Empowerment.

What I did not understand when I first named them was where they came from. I thought I had traced them from the pattern of restoration in Scripture. And I had — but only partially. The deeper I went, the more I realized these were not qualities to be built, earned, or even recovered.

They were already given.

Before a single Monday had ever existed. Before Adam had worked a day. Before Eve had made a single decision. On the sixth day, before the first week of human life was even complete, everything that H.A.V.E. describes had already been placed in human hands.

The H.A.V.E. Effect is not the reward at the end of the journey. It is the inheritance you are returning to.

By the time you reach Part Five, you will understand exactly what was in those hands. And why closing the Sunday/Monday Gap is not the achievement of something new, but the restoration of something you were always meant to carry.

How to Read This Book

Before God placed a single human being in the garden, He spent six days building the conditions that would make human flourishing possible. He did not rush. He did not skip steps. He did not fill what He had not yet structured or built on what He had not yet prepared. Light before life. Foundation before filling. Order before abundance.

This book follows that same sequence.

Not because I planned it that way from the beginning. Because I discovered, as the material took shape, that the only order in which this journey can be made is the order God has always used to build anything, you cannot restore what you have not first seen clearly. You cannot rebuild what you have not yet named. You cannot receive what the structure you are carrying cannot yet hold.

Six parts. Six movements. The same method God used in six days.

Part One lays the foundation. Before the gap can be addressed, the original design must be seen as what God built in the beginning. What the human interior was designed for. What peace looks like when it is structurally intact. You cannot long for what you were never designed for — and Part One shows you exactly what you were designed for.

Part Two examines the structure after the fall. Not to produce guilt, but to produce precision. The fractured interior. The broken sequence. The human heart operates in disorder and mistakes the disorder for its permanent condition. You cannot rebuild what you cannot see, and Part Two makes the fracture visible.

Part Three names the pattern. The drift that widens the gap slowly and quietly. The reason clarity fades even when it arrives with genuine force. The Sunday/Monday Gap itself — what it is, what it costs, and why naming it precisely is the first real movement toward closing it.

Part Four begins the rebuilding. What it looks like to reorder the interior around the governing center God designed. What cooperation with that work requires. What begins to shift when the structure underneath starts to change. Not a method. A direction.

Part Five reveals the H.A.V.E. Effect. What emerges naturally in a life that has been genuinely rebuilt around the right foundation. Not four disciplines to practice. Four pieces of evidence that the gap is closing — and that what was given on the sixth day is finally being received.

Part Six brings the journey into the ordinary. Not elevation. Not arrival. The durable, daily reality of a person who has stopped dividing against themselves. What a life that holds together actually looks like from the inside — in the work, the relationships, the quiet Tuesday afternoon that nobody is watching.

Read it slowly. Not because it is difficult, but because the truths it contains are not primarily information to be processed. They are realities to be received. The gap did not open in a moment, and it will not close in one either. But the direction can change today. And a life moving in the right direction, however gradually, is already different from the life it was before.

A Word Before We Begin

I want to be honest with you about something before the first chapter.

I am not writing this book from the position of having fully arrived. And I want to go further than that, because saying it once as a disclaimer is not the same as meaning it.

There have been seasons since that parking lot moment when the gap returned — not as wide as before, but real. Seasons where I was teaching alignment on a Tuesday and feeling the drift in my own interior by Thursday. Seasons when the coaching calls went well, the ministry was moving, and the interior was quieter than I wanted anyone to know.

That is not a confession of failure. It is a description of what the journey looks like for the person inside it. And I believe you deserve to know that the man who wrote this book is not someone who found the formula, applied it perfectly, and is now writing from the other side of the gap. I am writing from inside the ongoing work of closing it. The rebuilding is real. The progress is real. The H.A.V.E. Effect is not a theory I developed in an office. It is the framework I have been living toward, returning to, and being sustained by through seasons that required more than I had in myself.

That tension — between knowing the truth and still being formed by it — is not a problem to be solved before you can help others. It is the condition of every honest person doing this work. The gap does not close all at once. It closes gradually, across seasons, through the sustained practice of returning to the center when the drift pulls. The person who understands that is more useful to the people they serve than the person who presents themselves as beyond the struggle.

What I can tell you with confidence is this: the gap is not your identity. The inconsistency is not your destiny. The distance between who you are on Sunday and who you are on Monday is not the permanent condition of your life. It is a structural problem with a structural solution, and the God who designed you for alignment is the same God who initiates the rebuilding.

He is not waiting for you to close the gap on your own. He is the one doing the work. Your part is to turn toward it and remain turned, even when the progress is slower than you hoped and the drift returns more often than you expected.

XIX

The gap has a name. And what replaces it has a name too.

You are about to begin the journey from the Sunday/Monday Gap toward the H.A.V.E. Effect — from a life divided against itself toward a life held together by alignment. From the exhaustion of trying to maintain on your own what only God can sustain, toward the settled, durable peace of a person whose interior has been rebuilt around the right center.

Hope. Abundance. Virtue. Empowerment.

Not as goals to be achieved.

As the natural result of a life that has finally come into alignment with the design it was always meant to carry.

That life is available to you.

It begins on the next page.

Part One

What God Built

I

Peace Was the Original Design

"In the beginning God created the heavens and the earth... and God said, 'Let there be light,' and there was light."— Genesis 1:1-4

Before God built anything, He spoke light.

Not life. Not structure. Not the abundance that would eventually fill every prepared space. Light came first. And the first thing light did was make a distinction between what was illuminated and what was not. Between order and void. Between what God was building and what He was building it out of.

This was not incidental. It was the method.

Everything God creates, He first illuminates. He does not fill what He has not first made visible. He does not build on what He has not first distinguished from the chaos around it. Light is always the first movement — not because it is the most dramatic, but because without it, nothing that follows can be seen, named, or sustained.

This matters for the life you are trying to live. Because the gap between who you are on Sunday and who you are on Monday is not primarily a motivation problem or a discipline problem. It is a visibility problem. Something in the interior has gone dark. And you cannot rebuild what you cannot see.

God's first act in creation was illumination. His first act in restoration is the same.

That is where this book begins.

And for most believers, the place where the light has gone out is somewhere between Sunday morning and Monday afternoon.

Most people do not drift all at once. They drift from Monday to Monday.

They sit in a service on Sunday morning, and something real happens. The worship reaches a place in them that they forgot existed. A verse lands with a weight that feels like God pressing His finger directly on the wound. Clarity arrives. Peace settles. For an hour, maybe two, life feels ordered. Like everything makes sense, like they know exactly who they are and why they're here.

And then Monday comes.

The inbox. The commute. The tension at work didn't resolve over the weekend. The financial pressure that existed before Sunday and persists after it. The familiar weight of ordinary life returning. And the clarity — the peace that felt so solid twelve hours ago — is already starting to thin.

By Wednesday, some people can barely remember what they felt on Sunday. By Friday, they're wondering if they imagined it.

This pattern is more common than most people admit. And most people who experience it spend years assuming it's a personal failure. A discipline problem. A sign that something in them is spiritually insufficient. They try harder. They add more — more reading, more prayer, more commitment. They make and break promises to themselves about consistency. And the cycle repeats.

The problem is not their effort.

The problem is that they are trying to hold together a life whose inner architecture is still broken. And no amount of spiritual effort can substitute for structural restoration.

I want to tell you about a man I'll call Marcus.

Marcus had been in church his entire life. Grew up in a faith-filled home, gave his life to Christ at seventeen, married a woman who shared his convictions, and raised three children in the same tradition he had inherited. By every external measure, Marcus was a committed believer. He served on his church's leadership team. He led a small group on Thursday nights. He tithed consistently and prayed over his family every morning before they left for school.

But Marcus had a secret he had never said out loud to anyone.
He didn't feel any of it.

Not in the way he once had. Not in the way he watched other people in his congregation seem to feel it — the ones whose hands went up during worship with an ease that looked effortless, whose faces carried something during prayer that Marcus couldn't manufacture, no matter how hard he tried. He went through the motions with genuine sincerity. He believed the theology. He affirmed the doctrines. But somewhere between his head and his chest, something had gone quiet. And the more years that passed, the more he had come to accept the quiet as the permanent condition of his faith.

He sat across from me one afternoon and said something I have heard in different forms from more people than I can count:

"I don't know what's wrong with me. I do everything I'm supposed to do. I can't seem to hold onto it."

That phrase — I can't seem to hold onto it — is one of the most honest descriptions of the Sunday/Monday Gap I have ever heard. Not a crisis of belief. Not a dramatic falling away. Just the chronic, quiet experience of receiving something real on Sunday and watching it slip through your fingers before the week is out. Of knowing the truth intellectually and finding that it doesn't translate into the interior steadiness you thought it was supposed to produce.

Marcus was not spiritually deficient. He was structurally misaligned.

And the reason he couldn't hold onto what Sunday offered was not that he wasn't trying hard enough. It was that the inner architecture required to hold it had never been rebuilt. He was receiving something real into a vessel that had not yet been restored to the shape required to contain it.

That distinction — between a faith problem and a structural problem — is the most important distinction this book will ask you to make. Because the way you diagnose the problem determines the solutions you pursue. And if you spend twenty years treating a structural problem as a faith problem, you will spend twenty years wondering why the solutions keep failing.

Peace is not primarily a feeling. Peace is the result of order.

To understand what broke, we have to understand what was whole.

That requires going back. Not to the beginning of your story, but to the beginning of the human story. To a moment before disorder existed. To a condition of life so different from the one we now inhabit that it takes real effort to imagine it — and even more to believe it was always meant to be normal.

Genesis opens with a God who creates in sequence.

Light before life. Structure before abundance. Order before fruitfulness. Every element of the creation narrative follows the same pattern: God establishes the framework first, then fills it. He forms, then fills. He orders, then blesses. He structures, then multiplies.

This sequence is not arbitrary. It is the signature of how God builds anything — and it has direct implications for how He rebuilds the human interior.

On the first day, God did not create everything at once. He creates light. Separates it from darkness. Establishes the most fundamental distinction in existence — the difference between what is and what is not, between illumination and void — before anything else is made.

Notice what He does not do: He does not scatter light randomly into a formless environment and hope it organizes itself. He speaks light into being and immediately establishes a governing distinction between light and dark. Before anything can grow, the most basic condition for growth must be present.

On the second day, He separates the waters. Creates the sky. Establishes a boundary between what is above and what is below. More structure. More definition. More order carved out of formlessness. The environment is being prepared — not yet filled, only structured. God is in no hurry to fill what He has not yet ordered.

On the third day, the dry land appears. The seas are gathered. Vegetation begins to grow — not scattered randomly across a chaotic landscape, but organized by kind, bearing seed and reproducing according to design. Everything in its category. Everything expresses its nature within the structure that holds it.

Only then — once the framework is established, once the structure is in place — do the creatures appear. The birds of the air on the fifth day. The animals of the land on the sixth. And finally, at the culmination of the sequence, the human being.

What is God demonstrating across these six days? Not simply His creative power. His method. He is showing us that abundance never precedes order. That fruitfulness never stands where structure is absent. That everything which flourishes does so because it is aligned with the design beneath it. God does not scatter seeds onto unprepared ground and hope that something will grow. He prepares the ground. He always prepares the ground first.

This matters for the human interior in ways that go beyond the poetry of the creation account. If God builds everything — visible creation, the community of faith, the redeemed human soul — by establishing structure before filling it, then the experience of trying to sustain abundance without first restoring order is not just difficult; it is impossible. It is working against the grain of how God builds anything. The clarity that leaks out by Wednesday is not leaking through insufficient effort. It is leaking through the cracks of a structure that has not yet been rebuilt to hold it.

God does not scatter seeds onto unprepared ground and hope that something will grow. He prepares the ground first. He always does.

The apostle Paul captured something of this when he wrote of Christ: "All things were created through him and for him... and in him all things hold together." God did not just make the creation. God holds it together. Every element of existence operates within a structure that sustains it. Remove the structure, and everything falls apart. Maintain it and everything coheres.

When God surveys the completed creation and declares it very good, that phrase carries more theological weight than casual reading suggests. The

Hebrew word tov does not simply mean 'beautiful' or 'pleasant'. It means whole. Integrated. Functioning exactly as it was designed to function. Every element is in the right relationship with every other element. Nothing is working against its own design. Nothing is straining to maintain what should be effortless.

Creation, in that moment, was not just impressive; it was awe-inspiring. It was coherent.

And the Hebrew word underneath that coherence — the word the Old Testament uses repeatedly to describe the condition God intends for human beings — is shalom.

Shalom is routinely translated as 'peace,' but the English word lacks sufficient structural weight to convey what the Hebrew says. *Shalom* means completeness. Wholeness. The condition of a thing that has all its parts in their right relationship to one another. When the Old Testament writers used shalom to describe God's intention for human life, they were not describing the absence of conflict or the presence of pleasant feelings. They were describing the condition of a life in which everything is where it is supposed to be — rightly ordered, rightly related, functioning as designed.

The God who created in sequence, who ordered before filling, who structured before blessing, designed human beings to inhabit shalom as their natural condition. Not as a reward to be earned or a spiritual achievement to be reached. As the original operating environment of the human soul. The state that was normal before normal got interrupted.

The apostle Paul also wrote that God is not the author of confusion but of peace. That statement is often read as a source of comfort in difficult moments. It is, more precisely, a structural claim. Confusion is the symptom of disorder. Peace is the symptom of order. When life is structured the way God intended, peace is not something you have to fight for. It is simply what existence feels like from the inside.

The Hebrew word translated as Eden means delight. Pleasure. Not merely provision — delight.

God did not construct a minimal survival environment and place humanity inside it. He designed an atmosphere. He planted a garden — and the word planted suggests intention, cultivation, and care. Something a craftsman does with attention to detail. Something a father does for a child he wants to thrive.

He filled it with trees that were both beautiful to look at and nourishing to eat. Form and function are woven together. A river flowed through the garden and divided into four rivers, passing through lands filled with gold and precious stones. Resources Adam and Eve did not need to survive. God placed them there anyway. This is the signature of a God whose instinct is not sufficiency but abundance.

When God forms the seas, He doesn't make shallow ponds — He carves deep oceans. When He scatters stars across the sky, He doesn't hang a few for decoration — He fills the universe with billions of galaxies, each containing billions of stars, most of which no human eye will ever see. When He creates a garden for human beings to inhabit, He doesn't give them just enough. He gives them more than enough.

This matters because it directly addresses one of the most common distortions in how people think about the spiritual life: the idea that God is fundamentally conservative with His provision. That access to Him is rationed. That peace and clarity and interior steadiness are distributed sparingly to those who have done sufficient spiritual work to earn them.

That is not the God of Genesis 1.

The God of Genesis 1 creates a universe of staggering excess and places human beings at its center, not as stewards of scarcity but as heirs of abundance. The first thing God does after creating human beings is bless them. Do not instruct them. Do not warn them. Bless them. Before they have done a single thing, before they have demonstrated faithfulness or consistency or spiritual depth, God's first act toward them is to pour out blessing.

That is who He is. And that character does not change between Genesis 1 and the present moment. The scarcity is not coming from Him.

God's first act toward human beings was not instruction. It was a blessing.

And not merely in the material sense. Every dimension of their existence was abundant. Purposeful work without being exhausting. Relationships without rivalry or the insecurity that turns closeness into competition. Identity without the anxiety of needing to prove or protect it. Access to God Himself — not in a temple, not through an intermediary, not at designated hours of devotion, but in the ordinary rhythm of the day.

In the cool of the day, they walked with God.

Not in a sanctuary. Not in a designated spiritual moment set apart from the rest of life. In the cool of the day — in the ordinary flow of ordinary life. The walk with God was not the exception to their existence. It was the texture of it. Not something they scheduled or prepared for or attempted to manufacture through sufficient spiritual effort. Simply what happened when the day reached its most pleasant hour.

That is what shalom looks like when it is fully intact. Not a life where God appears in the designated moments and is absent from the rest. A life where the presence of God is the continuous atmosphere in which everything else occurs. Eden was not a reward. It was the architecture of human flourishing — the environment in which we were built to live, the conditions under which the human soul was designed to operate.

We were not made for the world we currently inhabit.

We were made for that one.

There is a dimension of the Eden narrative that most readers pass over too quickly. It has to do with the interior architecture of the human being — the specific order in which the human person was designed to function on the inside.

The Scriptures describe the human being as spirit, soul, and body. Not three separate entities coexisting inside the same skin, but three dimensions of a single person — each with a distinct function, each designed to operate in a specific relationship to the others.

The spirit is the deepest part of the human person. It is the capacity for direct communion with God — the part of us that was breathed into existence by God Himself when He formed Adam from the dust and breathed into his nostrils the breath of life. The Hebrew word for that breath is *neshamah* — the divine breath, the animating presence of God deposited into human clay. The spirit is what makes the human being categorically different from every other creature in the creation account. The animals were spoken into existence. The human being was breathed into existence. The spirit is where that distinction lives.

The soul is the seat of the mind, will, and emotions. It is where thinking happens, where decisions are made, where feelings are felt and processed. The soul is the part of the human person that encounters the world, interprets it, and responds to it. It is personal, particular, shaped by experience and memory, and the accumulated weight of everything a person has lived through.

The body is the physical instrument through which the inner life expresses itself in the world. It is the outermost dimension — the part that is visible, measurable, that occupies space and moves through time.

Before the fall, these three dimensions of the human person operated in a specific sequence. The spirit, in direct and unobstructed communion with God, governed the soul. The soul, receiving its orientation from the spirit, processed the world through a lens of clarity, trust, and divine wisdom rather than fear or self-protection. And the body expressed the life flowing through that ordered interior with a quality of presence and ease that had nothing to perform and nothing to manage.

Spirit leading. Soul following. Body expressing.

This sequence is not a theological abstraction. It is the description of what happens in the interior of a human being when everything is functioning as designed. And the effects of that sequence are immediately visible in the quality of life it produces.

When the spirit governs, the mind is clear. Not because life is simple or circumstances are easy, but because the governing center from which the mind operates is connected to the source of all wisdom and clarity. Confusion is not the baseline state. Order is. When a difficult situation arises, the soul that is following the spirit's lead processes it from a position of grounded confidence rather than anxious reactivity. The question is not whether I can handle this. It is what is the wise response to this, and the spirit already has access to the answer.

When the spirit governs, the emotions are not suppressed — they are rightly ordered. Adam felt. He experienced delight in the garden, joy in Eve's presence, and satisfaction in the work God had given him. The emotions were fully present and fully expressed. But they were not governing. They were responding to what the spirit, connected to God, had already settled about. Fear did not drive the interior because there was nothing in the interior's governing layer to produce fear. Anxiety did not organize the day because the provision and presence of God were not in question.

When the spirit governs, the body moves through the world without the physical weight of unresolved interior conflict. The tension that accumulates in the body of a person whose soul is disordered — the tightened jaw, the shallow breath, the chronic low-grade vigilance that never fully releases — none of that existed in the pre-fall body. Not because Adam's body was physically different, but because the interior from which it operated was structured differently.

Spirit leading. Soul following. Body expressing. This is the architecture of the life God designed.

Adam's clarity didn't need to be rebuilt every morning. His identity didn't require weekly reinforcement. His sense of direction didn't fade when circumstances became difficult or when the demands of the day multiplied. These things held not because Adam was exceptionally disciplined or spiritually advanced, but because the architecture beneath them was intact. The structure was doing what structure does: sustaining the life built on it.

This is what the Sunday/Monday Gap is ultimately about. Not the gap between church attendance and secular activity. Not the gap between religious behavior and everyday behavior. The gap is interior. It is the distance between the condition your spirit was designed to inhabit and the condition your soul currently operates from. When that sequence is intact — spirit leading, soul following — Sunday's clarity does not evaporate by Monday, because what produced the clarity was not the Sunday environment. It was the interior order. And interior order does not change when the environment does.

On Sunday, something happens that briefly restores that interior sequence. The worship, the word, the communal orientation toward God — these create an environment in which the spirit rises and the soul, for a time, quiets enough to follow. The inner life settles into something closer to the order God intended. And for a few hours, you feel what alignment feels like.

Then Monday arrives. The environment changes. Pressure returns. The soul, which has spent most of its life operating outside of Eden's order, takes back the lead. The spirit's voice grows faint. The clarity thins. And you are back, once again, to striving for peace rather than living away from it.

This is not a discipline failure. It is a structural condition. And the solution is not more Sundays. The solution is the restoration of the interior order that makes Sunday's clarity sustainable throughout the rest of the week.

When life is ordered correctly, peace emerges naturally.
It does not have to be chased. It does not have to be
maintained. It simply is.

Adam was placed in the garden to work it and keep it.

Work existed before the fall. Before sin. Before the curse. Before the world started resisting human effort, that matters because it means work itself was not punishment. What the fall changed was not the existence of work but the interior condition from which work was done.

In Eden, Adam worked from abundance. His provision was guaranteed not by his productivity but by the generosity of the One who designed him. He wasn't producing to earn his place. He wasn't striving to maintain his security. He was expressing his design — partnering with God in something already generative, already fruitful, already blessed.

Adam went to work every day with no anxiety about whether his effort would be sufficient. No fear that the harvest might not come. No quiet competition with anyone else who might be doing the work better. No inner voice cataloguing his inadequacies and questioning whether he was genuinely cut out for what he had been given to do. The interior from which his work flowed was entirely free of the performance anxiety that most people carry so constantly that they no longer even notice it is there.

He worked from rest. Not toward rest. From it.

That distinction is one of the most radical ideas in the entire creation narrative. The goal of the restored life is not to learn to rest after sufficient effort. It is to learn to work from a position of rest that was always the starting point. Most believers have never experienced work like that. Not because it is impossible, but because it requires an interior condition that has not yet been restored. When the soul is disordered — when fear rather than faith governs the inner life — even meaningful work becomes exhausting. Not because the work itself is bad, but because the architecture it flows from is broken.

The believer who prays on Sunday with genuine trust and spends Monday performing from anxiety is not a hypocrite. They are a person experiencing what happens when the order that made Adam's work sustainable has not yet been rebuilt inside them. Their desire is real. Their effort is genuine. The structure is not yet restored.

When Adam first saw Eve, his response was one of the most quietly remarkable moments in the entire narrative.

He didn't calculate. He didn't assess what her presence meant for his own position or security. He didn't wonder whether her strengths would make his weaknesses more visible. He didn't manage his emotional response to avoid appearing vulnerable.

He celebrated.

"This at last is bone of my bones and flesh of my flesh."

There is no insecurity in that sentence. No quiet competition. No fear that her strength might diminish his own significance. No holding back. No management of how his response would be perceived. Her existence multiplied his joy rather than threatening his security. He was completely present to the moment, completely available to what it offered, because there was nothing in his interior consuming resources on self-protection.

And then the text offers a detail that is easy to read past: they were both naked and were not ashamed.

Perfect vulnerability. Perfect safety. Perfect trust.

In Eden, there was nothing to conceal. Not because Adam and Eve had achieved a level of spiritual maturity where they no longer needed self-protection, but because nothing in them was misaligned. They were fully known, fully seen, fully exposed — and fully at rest. The instinct to manage perception, to show the curated version while hiding the rest, had no ground to stand on. There was no gap between who they were and who they appeared to be.

No Sunday version and Monday version. No public self and private self. No carefully maintained exterior that required energy to sustain. One life, held together by order, expressed without reservation to God and to each other.

Consider what those costs in the world east of Eden. The energy most people expend managing the distance between their inner reality and their outward presentation is staggering. The exhaustion of performing consistency when the interior feels anything but consistent. The private weight of knowing what is happening inside while maintaining the appearance of having it together. The loneliness of being seen but not actually known, because what is known would not be safe to show.

All that energy, all of that management, all of that exhaustion — none of it existed in Eden. Not because Adam and Eve had suppressed their authentic selves in favor of a performed version, but because their authentic selves were fully aligned with their design. There was no gap between who they were and who they were supposed to be. And in the absence of that gap, the entire apparatus of self-protection became unnecessary.

---

*In Eden, there was no gap between who they were and
who they appeared to be. No Sunday version and
Monday version. One life, held together by order.*

I want to return to Marcus for a moment.

After that first conversation — the one where he said he couldn't seem
to hold onto it — we spent several more sessions going beneath the
surface of what he was experiencing. And what gradually emerged was a
picture of a man who had been trying for decades to close the gap
through his own efforts. More discipline. More structure. More
accountability. More ministry involvement. He had tried every tool
available to a sincere, committed believer, and each had produced the
same result: temporary improvement followed by a return to the
baseline.

What Marcus had never considered was that the baseline itself might be
the problem.

He had been assuming that the gap between Sunday's clarity and
Monday's reality was the result of insufficient effort applied to a problem
that was fundamentally solvable through more effort. He had never been
given a framework that suggested the gap was structural — that it was
not evidence of personal failing but of an interior condition that effort
alone was never equipped to fix.

When I introduced him to the Eden framework — to the idea that what
he was experiencing was not spiritual immaturity but the structural
condition of a human being living east of the garden, whose interior had

not yet been rebuilt to the order it was designed for — something shifted in him that I have seen shift in people many times since.

He wept.

Not from despair. From relief. The relief of a man who had been carrying a diagnosis of personal failure for thirty years and was finally being told that the diagnosis was wrong. The problem was real, but it was not what he thought it was. And that meant the solution was also different from what he had been attempting.

That shift — from shame to structural understanding — is not a small thing. It is, in many ways, the first step of the entire restoration.

You cannot rebuild what you cannot see. And you cannot see clearly what you have spent years misidentifying.

The gap is not evidence that you are broken beyond repair.

It is evidence that a specific structure has not yet been restored. And structures can be rebuilt.

This is the world the human being was built for.

Not as a spiritual destination reached after sufficient growth. Not as a reward for exceptional faithfulness or the exclusive experience of a particularly devoted few. As the original operating condition of the human soul. The factory defaulted. The state that was normal before normal got interrupted.

And something in you already knows this.

You know it every time genuine peace arrives — not the absence of difficulty, but the presence of something steady and unshakeable underneath it. You know it in those rare seasons when your inner life feels ordered, when Sunday's clarity didn't evaporate by Wednesday. When faith felt less like effort and more like something you were living from, when you moved through a difficult week without losing your footing.

Those moments are not accidents. They are not spiritual highs to be chased and inevitably lost.

They are echoes.

Your soul carries the memory of Eden. Not as a place you have been, but as a condition you were designed for. Not a nostalgic longing for something you once had, but a structural resonance with something you were built to inhabit. Every moment of genuine alignment — every time peace holds when it should have broken, every time clarity survives a Monday, every time you move through difficulty from steadiness rather than reaction — is a small foretaste of the life God originally designed for human beings. And intends to restore.

The longing you carry for a life that holds together is not wishful thinking. It is not spiritual ambition that exceeds what is realistically available to ordinary people in ordinary lives. It is the most honest thing about you. It is the soul recognizing the distance between where it is and where it was always meant to be. And that recognition is not a source of discouragement. It is the beginning of the journey back.

Because you cannot long for what you were never designed for.

The longing itself is evidence of the design.

Faith was never meant to live in moments. It was meant to structure life.

Here is the central claim of this book, stated plainly:

People do not struggle because they lack faith.

They struggle because their lives are structurally misaligned with their beliefs.

The Sunday/Monday Gap is not a discipline problem. It is not a commitment problem. It is not the result of spiritual immaturity or insufficient effort. It is the inevitable experience of a human being trying to sustain what only alignment can sustain — in a world that stopped supporting alignment the moment humanity walked out of Eden.

That changes everything about what the solution looks like.

The answer is not to try harder. The answer is not more spiritual activity layered on top of an inner life that is still, at its core, operating from the broken order introduced by the fall. The answer is not a better morning routine, a more disciplined structure, or a more accountable community — though each has its place. The answer is restoration—the reordering of the interior life around the governing center it was always designed for.

Not self-improvement. Reordering.

God is not asking you to manufacture the peace that Adam had. He is not asking you to white-knuckle your way to the experience of a restored interior through sufficient spiritual effort. He is offering to rebuild, inside you, the conditions that made Adam's peace possible. That is not a project you undertake alone. It is something you participate in as God initiates and sustains the work. Your part is not effort. Your part is cooperation.

That is what this book is about. That is the journey every chapter traces.

But before we can understand how order gets rebuilt, we must understand what happened when it broke. Because what entered the human story on the day everything changed did not stay in the garden. It followed the human race out. It reshaped the interior architecture for everyone who came after. And it has been shaping the human condition — and the experience of believers trying to live faithfully in the gap between Sunday and Monday — ever since.

That is where the next chapter begins.

II

The Architecture of the Human Soul

"The heart is deceitful above all things and beyond cure. Who can understand it?" — Jeremiah 17:9

On the second day, God built boundaries.

Not because boundaries are restrictive. Because without them, nothing can hold its shape. He separated the waters above from the waters below. Established the firmament — a structural boundary between what belongs in one place and what belongs in another. Before life could fill the created order, the architecture that would contain and sustain that life had to be in place.

Day 2 was not dramatic. There were no creatures yet. No vegetation. No light splitting into color across the horizon. Just structure. Quiet, unglamorous, essential structure. The kind of work that never gets celebrated because it is invisible once the building is complete — and catastrophic when it is absent.

God built the architecture before He built anything else.

He did the same thing with the human being.

Before the garden. Before work. Before Eve. Before the first Monday had ever existed, God designed the human interior with a specific architecture. Not randomly. Not as an afterthought. With the same intentional sequencing He brought to the firmament. What he built inside the human being was not just a collection of capacities. It was a governing order—a structure designed to hold everything that would fill it.

Understanding that architecture is not optional for the person who wants to understand the Sunday/Monday Gap. Because the gap is not a motivational, disciplinary, or faith problem, it is an architectural problem. And you cannot fix what you have never properly seen.

This chapter shows you the architecture that God designed and what it was meant to do. And what it looks and feels like from the inside when the structure isn't functioning as it was built to.

The next chapter will explain why it so often isn't.

I want to tell you about a man I'll call David.

David had been following God since his early twenties. He had grown up in the church, walked away for a few years in his late teens, and come back with the kind of conviction that only people who have been genuinely lost seem to carry. He knew what it felt like to be without God. He did not take the return lightly.

For years, that conviction held. His faith was visible, grounded, and real. People in his church recognized something in him — a depth of sincerity, a hunger for the things of God that stood out. He led a small group. He mentored younger men. He was, by every external measure, one of those people whose faith seemed to be producing exactly what faith is supposed to produce.

But something had been shifting underneath all of that, so slowly that David had not noticed it.

It started with a season of failure — a business that collapsed, a relationship that fractured, a period when the things he had believed God was directing him toward seemed to lead nowhere good. He had prayed with confidence. He had stepped out in faith. And then watched things fall apart in ways he could not explain.

He told me, "I started questioning everything. Not God's existence. Something harder than that. Whether he was for me."

That question, once it arrived, settled into David's interior like sediment. He could not shake it in prayer because prayer itself had become the evidence of the problem — he had prayed, and the outcome had not matched what he believed he had been promised. He could not resolve it through Scripture because the same verses that had once arrived with clarity now seemed to have a distance to them, as if they were addressed to someone else. He continued showing up. He continued leading. But the interior certainty that had once made the showing up feel natural had been replaced by something quieter, colder, and far more exhausting.

He was not questioning God's power. He was questioning his own place within it.

The enemy had not needed to attack David's theology. He had waited for the season of loss, and then used it to introduce a single, persistent question into the architecture of David's identity: What if God moves for other people, but not for you?

That question does not announce itself as a lie. It arrives dressed as evidence. It uses real events, real disappointments, real gaps between what was believed and what was experienced, and it builds a case. Slowly. Patiently. The kind of case that does not feel like an accusation but like an honest assessment.

And it was breaking David from the inside out, in ways none of the people watching him lead, mentor, and serve had any idea what was happening.

When I told him that what he was experiencing was not evidence of something fundamentally wrong with him — not a verdict on his character, his faith, or his standing before God — but a structural condition, a fracture in the interior architecture that every human being carries and that seasons of loss have a particular way of activating, he was quiet for a long time.

Then he said, "I thought if I kept serving, nobody would know. Including me."

That sentence captures something true about what happens when the interior architecture fails to function as designed. It not only produces struggle. It teaches you to hide the struggle.

But before we can understand what happened to David's interior, we need to understand what God built it to be. Because you cannot identify a structural failure in something whose original design you have never seen.

The Scriptures describe the human being as spirit, soul, and body. Not three separate entities coexisting inside the same skin — but three dimensions of a single person, each with a distinct function, each designed to operate in a specific relationship with the others.

The spirit is the deepest part of the human person. It is the capacity for direct communion with God — the part of us that was breathed into existence when God formed Adam from the dust and breathed into his nostrils the breath of life. The Hebrew word for that breath is *neshamah* — the divine breath, the animating presence of God deposited into human clay. The spirit is what makes the human being categorically different from every other creature in the creation account. The animals were spoken into existence. The human being was breathed into existence. The spirit is where that distinction lives.

The soul is the seat of the mind, will, and emotions. It is where thinking happens, where decisions are made, where feelings are felt and processed. The soul is the part of the human person that encounters the world, interprets it, and responds to it. It is personal, particular, shaped by experience and memory, and the accumulated weight of everything a person has lived through.

The body is the physical instrument through which the inner life expresses itself in the world. It is the outermost dimension — the part that is visible, measurable, that occupies space and moves through time.

God designed these three dimensions to operate in a specific sequence. The spirit, in direct and unobstructed communion with God, governs the soul. The soul, guided by the spirit, processes the world through a lens of clarity, trust, and divine wisdom rather than fear or self-protection. And the body expresses the life flowing through that ordered interior with a quality of presence and ease that has nothing to perform or manage.

Spirit leading. Soul following. Body expressing.

This is not a theological abstraction. It is the description of what happens in the interior of a human being when the architecture is functioning as designed. And the effects of that sequence are immediately visible in the quality of life it produces.

When the spirit governs, the mind is clear. Not because life is simple or circumstances are easy, but because the governing center from which the mind operates is connected to the source of all wisdom and clarity. Confusion is not the baseline state. Order is. When a difficult situation arises, the soul that is following the spirit's lead processes it from a position of grounded confidence rather than anxious reactivity. The question is not whether I can handle this. It is what is the wise response to this, and the spirit already has access to the answer.

When the spirit governs, the emotions are not suppressed — they are rightly ordered. Adam felt. He experienced delight in the garden, joy in Eve's presence, and satisfaction in the work God had given him. The emotions were fully present and fully expressed. But they were not governing. They were responding to what the spirit, connected to God, had already settled about. Fear did not drive the interior because there was nothing in the governing layer to produce fear. Anxiety did not organize the day because the provision and presence of God were not in question.

When the spirit governs, the body moves through the world without the physical weight of unresolved interior conflict. The tightened jaw, the shallow breath, the chronic low-grade vigilance that never fully releases — none of that exists when the interior from which the body operates is structured correctly. Not because the body is different. Because the architecture above it is intact.

This is the firmament God built inside every human being. A governing structure designed to hold the life that fills it. Spirit at the top. Soul in the middle. Body at the expression. Each layer does what it was designed to do, in the order it was designed.

When that sequence is intact, clarity does not need to be rebuilt every Monday morning. Identity does not require weekly reinforcement. Peace does not evaporate when the environment changes. Not because the person is exceptionally disciplined or spiritually advanced. Because the architecture beneath them is holding.

The human soul was not designed to govern itself. It was designed to be governed by the spirit. And the spirit was designed to be governed by God.

That sequence is the entire architecture. When it is intact, everything above it remains in place. When it is not, everything above it — the decisions, the emotions, the relationships, the work, the faith — becomes harder to sustain than it was ever meant to be.

The prophet Jeremiah wrote one of the most unsettling sentences in all of Scripture:

"The heart is deceitful above all things and beyond cure. Who can understand it?"

Most people read that verse as a warning about moral corruption. A reminder that the human heart tends toward sin and should not be trusted. And that reading is not wrong. But it misses the deeper diagnostic truth Jeremiah was naming.

The word translated "deceitful" in Hebrew is *'aqob* — from a root meaning crooked, or bent at the heel. It carries the sense of something that deviates from its intended line. Not necessarily in a dramatic direction. Sometimes just a degree or two off. But sustained over distance, a degree or two off from the true line produces a significant divergence.

Jeremiah was not primarily describing a heart that lies to other people. He was describing a heart that cannot fully trust its own perceptions.

That misreads reality. That interprets the world through a lens it doesn't know is distorted. A heart that feels certain about conclusions that are, in fact, the product of a bent interior working from disordered information.

This is what happens when the architectural sequence is reversed. When the soul moves to the governing position it was never designed to occupy, it does not simply perform less well; it performs worse. It begins to misread everything. God's silence reads as disinterest. His timing reads as neglect. Difficulty reads as abandonment. The soul operating from the front is not equipped to interpret reality accurately — because it was never designed to lead. It was designed to follow.

The human heart is not empty. It is divided.

The question Jeremiah asks at the end of that verse is as important as the statement before it: "Who can understand it?" He is not asking rhetorically. He is identifying a genuine problem. The fractured heart cannot fully diagnose itself. The instrument of perception is itself distorted. A bent ruler cannot accurately measure its own bending. A soul operating out of sequence cannot fully see its own disorder.

This is why David could lead, mentor, and serve for months while the interior collapse was happening without being able to name what was wrong. Not because he was in denial. Because the thing he was using to assess his interior was the same thing that had been displaced, he kept evaluating himself through the lens of the disorder. The disorder kept producing conclusions that felt like self-knowledge but were actually self-misdiagnosis.

This is why so many believers spend years trying to fix the wrong things. They identify the symptoms — the anxiety, inconsistency, the cycles of collapse and recommitment — and address them directly. They work on discipline. They develop better habits. They commit more seriously. And they make progress, sometimes significant progress. But the deeper architectural disorder remains because the thing doing the diagnosing is the thing that is out of sequence.

Only God can see the human heart clearly from the outside and still move toward it with restoration rather than condemnation. That is precisely what He does.

The apostle Paul described the interior experience of architectural disorder with a candor that has surprised readers for two thousand years.

"For I do not understand what I do. For what I want to do I do not do, but what I hate I do."

This is not the confession of a man with weak faith. Paul wrote this after his encounter with Christ on the road to Damascus. After years of ministry. After planting churches across the Roman world and enduring imprisonment, beatings, and shipwreck for the sake of the gospel. He was not a spiritual beginner; he described his struggles with temptation.

He was a mature believer describing something that persisted beneath all of that. Something that did not resolve through greater commitment or more disciplined practice.

I have the desire to do what is good, but I cannot carry it out.

The problem Paul identifies is not desire. His desire was genuine. The problem is the gap between desire and execution. Between what he wanted to do and what actually happened. Between intention and outcome.

That gap is the architecture not holding.

Paul goes further. He describes the experience not just as a gap but as a conflict.

"For in my inner being I delight in God's law; but I see another law at work in me, waging war against the law of my mind and making me a prisoner."

War. Not weakness. Not a lack of discipline. Not insufficient commitment. War.

This is what the interior sounds like when the spirit and soul are pulling in opposite directions. One part — the spirit, in communion with God — knows what is true and desires to live by it. Another part — the soul, operating from the front without the spirit's governing influence — pulls toward self-protection, fear, and the familiar patterns of a life lived from disorder. Both are real. Both are present. And without restoration of the inner architecture, neither wins decisively.

David experienced this war in the months after his season of loss. The part of him that had known God for years, that had built real history with Him, that recognized the enemy's voice even while struggling to resist it — that part was still present and still fighting. It never fully disappeared. But the part operating from the disorder — from the accumulated evidence of unanswered prayers and collapsed expectations — was fighting just as hard in the other direction. And on most Mondays, through most ordinary weeks, the war left him too exhausted to feel like either side was winning.

The result is the inconsistency most believers know far better than they are willing to admit.

James identified the same reality with a phrase that has become so familiar it has almost lost its force:

"A double-minded man is unstable in all his ways."

Double-minded. The Greek word is *dipsuchos* — literally, two-souled. A person is divided at the center and pulled in two directions by two different governing orientations that cannot lead at once.

The double-minded person is not insincere. They are not indifferent. They genuinely want to follow God. They genuinely desire alignment. But at the level of the inner architecture, two competing impulses are vying for the governing position. And because neither fully wins, the life that results is unstable. Not dramatically. Not catastrophically. Just... inconsistent.

Strong in certain moments. Fragile in others.

Clear on Sunday. Clouded by Wednesday.

Convicted after worship. Hesitant by Thursday afternoon.

James does not describe this person as rebellious. He describes them as unstable. Instability is not a moral failure — it is an architectural condition. A life being pulled by two different centers of gravity at once cannot hold a straight line. Doublemindedness is not a character flaw to be overcome through greater willpower. It is a structural problem that requires a different kind of solution.

The greatest conflict in the Christian life is often internal.

This is why the straightforward advice that fills most conversations about spiritual growth — "be more consistent," "develop better habits," "commit more deeply" — produces such limited and short-lived results for so many people.

You cannot discipline your way out of a divided architecture.

You can manage it. You can compensate for it. You can, through significant effort, hold it in check in some areas while it expresses itself in others. But the division itself remains. Until the architecture is restored to its designed sequence — spirit governing, soul following — the instability will continue.

It helps to be specific about what a disordered interior actually produces in daily life. Most people experience symptoms without recognizing the source.

It produces conviction without consistency. You receive truth. You feel genuinely moved by it. You intend to live differently. And then, without any dramatic decision to abandon that intention, you find yourself three weeks later in the same place you started. The conviction was real. The architecture swallowed it.

It produces clarity without retention. You experience a moment of genuine spiritual clarity — in worship, in prayer, in a conversation that opens something up — and it feels like everything has shifted. Like you can see exactly what needs to change and how. And then the week returns, and the clarity quietly dissolves under the weight of ordinary demands. Not because you rejected it. Because the soul that received it was not yet ordered to hold it.

It produces desire without direction. You want to follow God consistently. You want your faith to structure your entire life rather than appear only in weekly intervals. The desire is genuine. But desire alone cannot reconstruct interior architecture. Wanting to be aligned is not the same as being aligned. And the gap between those two realities — between wanting and being — is where most believers live in discouragement.

Clarity without structure cannot sustain itself.

It also produces a particular kind of fatigue distinct from ordinary tiredness. It is the exhaustion of holding an inner life together that keeps it from falling apart. Of managing the gap between who you appear to be and what is happening inside, and recommitting the same intentions repeatedly without the structural support to sustain them.

David knew this fatigue intimately. Not the tiredness of a man who had worked too hard or rested too little. The tiredness of a man who had been managing an internal war for months without anyone knowing the battle was happening—the smile at the front of the church. The encouragement dispensed to people who were struggling with things far smaller than what he was carrying. The morning prayers felt more like an obligation than a conversation. All of it maintained, all of it genuine in its way, all of it cost more than it should have because the interior that was supposed to be generating the energy had been quietly losing the fight.

Jesus spoke directly to people carrying that fatigue.

"Come to me, all who are weary and burdened, and I will give you rest."

The weariness He addressed was not primarily physical. It was the weariness of a disordered interior working too hard to hold itself together without the architecture that was always meant to hold it.

There is a dimension of the disordered interior that is rarely discussed with enough precision: what it does to the experience of intimacy with God.

The disordered soul does not prevent a person from believing in God. It does not block the spirit's genuine desire for Him. But it produces a chronic interference in the experience of nearness that most believers have quietly concluded is simply the normal texture of spiritual life.

The soul operating out of sequence relates to God from the same posture it brings to everything else: performance, management, and a low-grade anxiety about whether it is doing enough. Prayer becomes a report rather than a conversation. Worship becomes an activity rather than an encounter. Scripture becomes information to be processed rather than a living voice to be received.

None of this is insincere. The person doing it genuinely desires more. But the disordered interior has inserted its own patterns between the person and the God they are reaching toward, and those patterns filter the experience of nearness into something thinner and more effortful than it was designed to be.

This is why the same passage of Scripture can land differently on two different people. One person reads a verse, and something in them opens — the words arrive with weight and aliveness, with a quality of being addressed directly. Another person reads the same verse and receives correct information, nothing more. The difference is not sincerity. It is the condition of the interior receiving it. The ordered soul is available to encounter. The disordered soul is available only to information.

David had been doing this for months without realizing it. He was still reading Scripture every morning and still praying. Still present in every form that mattered to anyone watching. But something essential had shifted in how he was experiencing those practices. They had become maintenance rather than communion. He was keeping the forms alive while the architectural disorder quietly widened beneath them.

---

*The disordered interior does not keep God at a
distance. It keeps the person from receiving the nearness
He is always offering.*

One of the most painful consequences of a disordered interior is its effect on a person's self-image.

When the soul operates outside its designed sequence, self-reflection becomes unreliable. The bent ruler cannot measure its own bending. So the person who experiences chronic inconsistency doesn't usually conclude that their interior architecture is out of order. They conclude that they are broken. That something is fundamentally wrong with them as a person that they lack the character, the discipline, or the faith that other people seem to have.

They turn a structural condition into an identity statement.

And identity statements are far harder to challenge than structural diagnoses, because they feel like truth rather than interpretation. "I'm just not a consistent person" feels like self-knowledge. It is actually self-misdiagnosis. The inconsistency is real. But its source is not character. It is architecture.

David had arrived at exactly this conclusion. The failure of his business, the fracturing of his relationship, the months of ministry performed over a hidden interior collapse — he had assembled all of it into a quiet verdict about himself that he had never spoken aloud but had never stopped believing. That he was the kind of person God used in certain seasons and passed over in others. That the confidence he had once carried in his calling was something he must have manufactured rather than received.

The enemy does not need to convince a person to abandon their faith. He only needs to convince them that faith doesn't apply to them the way it applies to others. That the promises are real, but not for you specifically. The inheritance exists, but you are not quite in the line of succession.

That lie does not feel like a lie. It feels like humility. Like honest self-assessment. Like the mature recognition that not everyone receives the same measure of grace.

It is one of the most effective strategies the adversary deploys against sincere believers — not because it attacks what they believe, but because it quietly erodes who they believe themselves to be within what they believe. And a person who has lost confidence in their own identity before God cannot access the full weight of what they theologically hold to be true. The belief remains. The inhabiting of it does not.

Jesus said something in the garden of Gethsemane that is worth sitting with in this context.

To His disciples, who had fallen asleep when He asked them to watch and pray, He said:

> *"The spirit indeed is willing, but the flesh is weak."*

He was not scolding them. He was naming a condition.

The spirit — the part of them that genuinely desired to be present, to honor the moment, to stand with their Lord in His most difficult hour — was willing. The desire was real. But the flesh — the body and soul operating out of the designed sequence — could not sustain it. Not because they lacked sincerity. Because the architecture was not yet restored.

That gap between the willing spirit and the weak flesh is the architectural disorder made visible. And it is not resolved by trying harder. The disciples could not have willed themselves into wakefulness through greater commitment to the moment. What they needed was a different interior order — one that would come to them after the resurrection, through the Spirit God would send to rebuild what had been reversed.

The willing spirit is not a lie. The genuine desire to follow God that lives in every sincere believer is real. It is the spirit, doing what the spirit was designed to do — reaching toward God, recognizing truth, responding to His presence.

The weak flesh is not evidence of insincerity. It is evidence of the architectural disorder. The soul and body, operating from the reversed sequence, pulling against what the spirit is reaching toward.

Both are real. Both are present. And the experience of living between them — the gap between what the spirit receives and what the soul can sustain — is not a spiritual crisis. It is a structural one with a structural solution.

The spirit longs for God. The flesh pulls in another direction. Understanding this reframes the entire experience of spiritual inconsistency.

The architectural disorder does not live only in the interior. It expresses itself through the body as well.

The Spirit–Soul–Body sequence was designed to flow in one direction. Spirit governing, soul processing, body expressing. When the sequence reverses, the body — now operates from a soul driven by fear rather than governed by the spirit — begins to carry what it was never designed to carry.

The person living in structural misalignment does not just feel spiritually thin; they feel spiritually empty. They often feel physically heavy. The accumulated weight of anxiety that never fully resolves. Tension that lives in the shoulders, the chest, and the jaw. The low-grade vigilance that a disordered soul keeps the body in as a constant operating mode. The body was designed to express peace. When the interior is not at peace, the body carries the difference.

Most people manage this physical expression of the disorder through the same strategies they apply to its spiritual dimensions: effort, discipline, and attempts to override, through willpower, what the structure keeps producing. These strategies produce real relief. But they address the expression of the disorder rather than the disorder itself.

When the interior begins to reorder — when spirit moves back to the governing position and the soul begins to follow rather than lead — the body begins to carry something different. The peace that returns to the interior does not stay contained there. It expresses itself through the body in the same way as the disorder did. The chronic tension becomes intermittent. The constant vigilance becomes occasional. The weight that seemed like a permanent feature of how life felt begins to lift gradually.

This is one of the most tangible signs that the rebuilding is real. Not just a change in spiritual experience or theological understanding, but a change in how it feels to be inside your own body on an ordinary Wednesday afternoon.

Here is what the architectural disorder is not:

It is not your identity.

It is not your destiny.

There is no evidence that you are beyond the reach of what God can do in a human life.

The disorder is a condition — real, deeply consequential, and shared by every human being who has ever tried to sustain clarity between Sunday and Monday. But conditions can be addressed. Structures can be rebuilt. The interior order that God designed can be restored. Not through discipline or willpower, but through a process of genuine reconstruction that God initiates and sustains.

David eventually found language for what had been happening to him. Not all at once. Not through a single dramatic breakthrough. But gradually, as the architectural disorder was named and the source of instability was identified, the war he had been losing in silence began to shift. Not because the circumstances that had broken his confidence changed — they largely didn't. But because the architecture beneath the circumstances began to be rebuilt by something more reliable than his own effort.

He told me, months later: "I stopped trying to feel certain and started letting God rebuild the foundation the certainty was supposed to rest on."

That is a man who has begun to understand the architecture — and begun to receive the restoration.

But there is one more thing that needs to be understood before the rebuilding can begin. We have seen the architecture God designed. We have seen what it looks and feels like when the sequence is reversed. What we have not yet answered is the question underneath all of it:

How did it get this way?

That is where the next chapter begins.

III

When Disorder Entered the Story

"Therefore the LORD God sent him out of the garden of Eden to work the ground from which he was taken." — Genesis 3:23

On the third day, God prepared the ground.

He gathered the seas into their place. Dry land appeared. And out of that prepared ground came vegetation — seed-bearing plants and fruit-bearing trees, each producing according to its own kind. The ground was not neutral. It was generative. Built to receive, to hold, and to multiply what was placed in it. God had made it that way deliberately. The fruitfulness of everything that came after depended on the integrity of the ground beneath it.

The ground was designed to sustain life. And for a time, it did.

Then came the moment that changed everything. And when God described the consequences of what Adam and Eve had done, the first thing He addressed was not their relationship, not their work, not their bodies. It was the ground.

"Cursed is the ground because of you."

The very thing God had prepared on Day 3 to sustain fruitfulness was the first casualty of disorder. Not because the ground had done anything wrong. Because the ground is always the first thing that changes when the architecture above it collapses.

This is still true inside human beings.

The interior ground — the soul, prepared and ordered by God to receive what the spirit deposits and multiply it into a fruitful life — is the first thing that changes when the architectural sequence reverses. Chapter 2 showed you the architecture God built: spirit governing, soul following, body expressing. This chapter shows you the moment when the sequence was reversed. What entered the human story? What it did to the ground. And why the effects of that moment are still shaping the experience of every person who has ever tried to carry Sunday's clarity into Monday's reality.

Everything was whole.

Then it wasn't.

The transition from Genesis 2 to Genesis 3 is one of the most jarring moments in all of Scripture — not because it is dramatic, but because it isn't. There is no warning. No slow deterioration. No season of wandering before the fall. One moment, Adam and Eve are living in seamless alignment with God and with each other, in a world that reflects His generous design at every level. The next moment, they hide from Him among the trees.

The speed of it tells us something important.

The fall was not primarily an event that happened outside of them. It was an event that happened inside them. And internal collapse — the kind that happens in the architecture of the soul, beneath the surface of behavior — can occur faster than we realize. Not always with fanfare. Sometimes, with nothing more than a shift in perspective.

A question.

A reframe.

A moment of choosing to see what you have through the lens of what you lack.

That is where the fall began. Not with the fruit. With a question designed to change how Adam and Eve saw what they already possessed.

I want to tell you about a woman I'll call Denise.

Denise had been serving in ministry for eleven years. Women's ministry coordinator, small group leader, volunteer coordinator, Sunday school teacher. If the church needed something done, Denise was the person who showed up. Not reluctantly — genuinely. She loved the work. She loved the people. She had built her entire adult life around the conviction that faithfulness meant availability, and she had been available for over a decade.

But by the time she sat across from me, something had broken.

She couldn't pinpoint when it happened. There was no dramatic moment, no crisis event, no single Sunday where everything changed. Just a slow, barely perceptible draining that she had been compensating for with effort until the effort itself was no longer producing anything. She still showed up. She still served. But the interior that had once made the serving feel like overflow was now running on fumes. She was giving out of a vessel that nothing was flowing into, and she had been doing it for so long that she could no longer distinguish between faithfulness and exhaustion.

She told me, "I used to feel God in the work. Now I feel tired."

She had not stopped believing. She had not walked away. She had simply given past her margins for long enough that her capacity for genuine fruitfulness had collapsed. Sunday would come, and something would stir — a moment in worship where the weight lifted briefly, where she remembered what it had felt like to serve from fullness. And then Monday would come, and the obligations would return, and by Wednesday, the Sunday moment felt like a mirage.

What was happening to Denise was not a faith crisis. It was a capacity crisis. Burnout had not begun in her body — it had begun in an unguarded interior that had kept saying yes long after the soul had nothing left to give. The enemy had not needed to tempt her with sin. He had used her own faithfulness against her, gradually eroding every

God-given margin until what remained was the performance of ministry without its power.

She had not stopped believing. She had not made a single decision to step back from God. She had passed every margin her soul had, for long enough that the vessel was empty, and she no longer knew what full felt like. The ground that had once been generative had become exhausted. Not from too little faith. From too little order.

When I named what she was experiencing not as a spiritual failure but as a structural one — as the predictable result of an interior running from empty rather than full, of a soul that had been giving without receiving long enough to forget what receiving felt like — she was quiet for a long moment.

Then she said, "I thought if I kept giving, God would keep filling. I didn't realize I had stopped letting Him."

It is one of the most common confusions in the Christian life. And it begins, as almost everything in the human condition begins, in the garden.

The serpent's strategy is worth examining carefully, because it is the same strategy still at work in the human soul today.

He did not begin with a command. He began with a question.

"Did God really say you shall not eat of any tree in the garden?"

God had said something very different. He had said they could freely eat from every tree in the garden — except one. The emphasis in God's original statement was freedom. Abundance. Permission. Out of an entire garden, one boundary.

The serpent inverted the frame.

He shifted the emphasis from the trees they could eat to the ones they could not. Same facts. Completely different perspective. In a single sentence, he transformed a world of abundance into a world of restriction.

This is not a small move. It is the foundational move of disorder. And it has been repeated in every human soul ever since.

Because once you begin to see the world through the lens of what you lack, the abundance that surrounds you becomes invisible. The garden did not change. God's provision did not diminish. But Eve's perception of it did. And perception, when it is disordered, reshapes everything.

Notice what the serpent did not do. He did not attack God's power. He did not deny God's existence. He did not even directly contradict what God had said. He introduced a question that made God's goodness seem uncertain. That made His provision seem conditional. That made the boundary seem like withholding rather than protection.

"God knows that when you eat of it, your eyes will be opened, and you will be like God."

The implication was clear: the boundary was not for your benefit. It was for His. God is holding something back. Something you need. Something that would make you more than you currently are.

In that moment, for the first time in human history, the soul looked at what it had and concluded it was not enough.

The absence of peace is often the presence of disorder.

That conclusion — I do not have enough, I am not enough, something essential is missing — is the root of every form of human striving that has existed since. And it entered the human story not through rebellion, but through a reframe. A single question that changed the lens through which everything was seen.

The attack was not against behavior. It was against the order. Not against morality. Against alignment. Not against what Adam and Eve did. Against how they saw.

This matters enormously for how we understand the disorder we experience today. Most people assume that what needs to change is their behavior. If they could do more of the right things and fewer of the wrong things, the gap would close. But behavior is downstream of perception. And perception is downstream of the governing center of the interior life.

The serpent knew this. He did not first address the behavior. He attacked the governing center. He reframed reality until the soul's perception of God shifted from trust to suspicion. And once that shift happened, the behavior followed inevitably.

It still works the same way.

The person who loses their peace on Monday has not usually made a dramatic decision to abandon their Sunday convictions. They have allowed the week's noise, pressure, and demands to reframe how they see their situation gradually. God's provision begins to seem conditional. The gap between where they are and where they want to be began to feel like evidence of God's withholding rather than His timing. And the soul, operating from that reframe, pulls away from the trust that Sunday had restored — not in a single dramatic moment, but in a hundred small ones, each barely noticeable, each moving in the same direction.

The serpent never needed a different strategy. The original one still works.

The fruit was not the fall.

It was the symptom of the fall.

The real collapse happened inside Eve before anything appeared in her hands. She looked at the tree and saw that it was "good for food, and a delight to the eyes, and was to be desired to make one wise." The tree had always been there. Its appearance had not changed. But her perception of it had shifted entirely. What had previously been off-limits had become, in her mind, a deprivation she was being denied rather than a boundary she was being protected by.
She stepped out of the divine sequence.

Adam, who was with her, stepped out of the divine covering.

And in that moment, the interior architecture that had defined human existence — spirit leading, soul following, body expressing — reversed. The soul, inflamed by desire and disconnected from the spirit's governing influence, made a unilateral decision. The body followed. And the spirit, suddenly cut off from the unmediated communion with God that had sustained it, fell silent under the weight of what had just happened.

Everything that followed was immediate.

And in the immediacy of what followed, we can see the exact shape of what disorder does to the human person. Not as abstract theology. As a diagnostic picture of what happens inside every person whose interior architecture has not yet been restored to the sequence God designed.

The first symptom was shame.

"Then the eyes of both of them were opened, and they realized they were naked."

They had always been naked. Nothing physically had changed. But something internal had shifted so completely that the same reality now felt unbearable. Where once there was nothing to hide, now there was everything to hide. The soul that had lived in perfect transparency before God and each other now felt exposed and unsafe.

Shame is what the soul feels when it knows it has stepped outside of the order it was designed for. It is the interior signal that alignment has been broken. Not a feeling to be managed or suppressed, but a diagnostic indicator pointing to a structural reality.

They sewed fig leaves together and covered themselves. The coverings were inadequate — they knew it — but the instinct was immediate. When the inner life loses alignment with God, the reflex is concealment. We cover the gap between who we appear to be and what is happening inside. We manage the presentation. We show the Sunday version and protect the Monday version from view.

That instinct began in this moment. And it has never stopped.

The problem with fig leaves is not just that they are inadequate; they are also dangerous. It is that they confirm the disorder rather than addressing it. They treat the symptom — the exposed feeling — without touching the structural condition that produced it. You can wear fig leaves for years and still be just as exposed underneath them as the day you first reached for them.

Most believers know this from experience. The performance of spiritual consistency, maintained faithfully over the years, while the interior remains quietly disordered. The Sunday presentation, polished and genuine seeming, covers a weekday reality that tells a different story. Not hypocrisy in the cynical sense — the desire for the Sunday version to be real is genuine. But a structural gap between what is presented and what is lived that no amount of effort at the presentation level can close.

Small misalignments, repeated daily, eventually create large distances.

The second symptom was fear.

They heard God walking in the garden in the cool of the day. The same sound that had once been the most natural and welcome part of their existence. The sound of the One who made them, moving through the world He had built for them.

And they hid.

For the first time in the history of creation, human beings were afraid of God.

This is one of the most theologically significant details in the entire narrative. God had not changed. His character had not shifted. His intentions toward Adam and Eve were exactly what they had always been. But the interior disorder that now lived in them made His presence feel like a threat rather than a gift. The same reality — God approaching, God near — that had once been the source of their deepest peace now produced their deepest fear.

When God called out — "Where are you?" — it was not because He did not know. It was because Adam needed to hear his answer. And Adam's answer reveals the full shape of what had entered him:

"I heard the sound of you in the garden, and I was afraid, because I was naked, and I hid myself."

Fear. Exposure. Hiding. Three things that were never meant to exist in the human experience of God.

Three things that now live in every soul whose interior architecture has not yet been restored to order.

Consider how this expresses itself in the modern believer's experience. The person who approaches prayer with a low-grade anxiety about whether they have done enough to deserve to be heard. The one who avoids Scripture in seasons of failure because reading it feels like confronting a judge rather than meeting a father. The one who can worship freely on Sunday when surrounded by others but finds personal intimacy with God stilted and uncomfortable in the privacy of Monday, because in the absence of the community environment, the disordered soul's fear of exposure reasserts itself and the presence of God feels less like welcome and more like examination.

The fear Adam felt in the garden was the first Sunday/Monday Gap. God approaching in the cool of the day was a Sunday moment. Adam's hiding was Monday's response. The same God. The same garden. But an interior so altered by disorder that the relationship that had once been effortless was now experienced as threatening.

That pattern has repeated itself in every human soul ever since.

The third symptom was blame.

When God asked Adam what had happened, Adam did not take responsibility. He deflected.

"The woman whom you gave to be with me — she gave me fruit of the tree, and I ate."

The sentence contains two redirections. The first toward Eve. The second, more subtle, toward God Himself: "the woman whom you gave to be with me." Adam was not merely blaming Eve. He was implicating the One who had brought her into his life.

The man who had celebrated Eve's existence with unguarded joy — "this at last is bone of my bones" — was now positioning her as the explanation for his failure.

The relationship that had been built entirely on celebration now carried suspicion. The trust that had made perfect vulnerability possible now had a crack.

This is what disorder does to relationships. It does not stay contained to the interior life. It spreads outward. When the soul is operating from fear and self-protection rather than security and abundance, the people closest to you become either shields or threats. The instinct shifts from partnership to self-preservation. The energy that once went into building the relationship is redirected into protecting yourself within it.

And the deflection itself — the blame, the external explanation for the internal condition — is one of the most reliable indicators that the soul is operating from disorder. The ordered interior takes responsibility because it operates from a sense of security. It does not need to deflect, as its sense of identity is not threatened by acknowledging failure. But the disordered interior deflects instinctively, because admitting the failure feels like losing the last line of defense.

The fracture that began in Adam's inner world immediately expressed itself in his closest relationship. It still works that way.

After the confrontation in the garden, God described the world that Adam and Eve were now entering. And the description reveals something important about what had changed — not just around them, but in them.

"Cursed is the ground because of you; through painful toil you will eat food from it all the days of your life. It will produce thorns and thistles for you."

Work had existed in Eden. But Eden's work had flowed from a specific interior condition — abundance, security, the ease of a soul operating in divine order. Outside Eden, that interior condition was broken. And when the inner architecture is reversed, the same work that once energized now exhausts. The same responsibilities that once felt like a partnership now feel like a burden.

The ground did not become hostile to human effort because God was punishing the ground. It became resistant because the human being trying to work was now operating from a state of disorder rather than alignment. Resistance was the world reflecting the condition of the soul inside it.

This is still true. The same task can feel entirely different depending on the condition of the interior from which it is approached. Work done from peace feels purposeful. Work done from anxiety feels endless. Work done from a soul that is connected to its design and secure in its provision has a quality of flow that is almost unrecognizable to the person performing the same work from a soul driven by fear.

Denise had been experiencing this for years without having a language for it. The work had not changed. The people had not changed. The calling had not changed. But the interior from which she was doing the work had been gradually losing its alignment, and the ground had been reflecting that loss to her in the form of exhaustion, emptiness, and the creeping sense that what had once been fruitful had become merely functional.

The cursed ground is not only outside us. It is the interior condition of a soul working from disorder rather than design.

The greatest spiritual danger is not collapse. It is a gradual drift.

Most people, when they feel that exhaustion, assume they need to work harder. Or rest more. Or find a better strategy. What they actually need is restored order.

But there was one more detail in God's response to the fall that is easily missed — and it tells us everything about what comes next.

Before sending Adam and Eve out of the garden, God clothed them.

He replaced their inadequate coverings with something that held.

It was a small act. But it was a profound signal. The coverings God provided were made from animal skins, which means something had to die to cover what the fall had exposed. This is not incidental. It is the first picture in Scripture of the principle that runs through the entire biblical narrative and finds its fullest expression in the cross: the gap between the disordered human condition and the ordered life God designed is covered not by human effort, but by substitutionary provision— something given in place of what was lost.

God was the first one to cover the gap between who they had become and who they were designed to be. The soul's instinct was to hide. God's instinct was to cover — not to deny the disorder, but to restore what disorder had stripped away.

The pattern of restoration was established in the very moment of the fall. God always moves first toward what has been lost. And His moving is never merely emotional. It is structural. He does not simply forgive the disorder. He begins the work of covering it, addressing it, and ultimately reversing it.

That work did not end at the garden gate. It followed Adam and Eve out.

It followed the entire human race.

And it is still following you.

What happened in the garden did not remain in the garden.

The interior architecture that fractured in Adam and Eve became the inherited condition of every human being who came after them. The apostle Paul would write centuries later: "Sin entered the world through one man, and death through sin, and in this way, death came to all people." The consequence of what happened in Eden was not merely personal — it was structural. It became part of the design of the human experience itself.

Every person born east of Eden enters the world with the reversed sequence already in place—soul leading. Spirit muffled. The body is reacting to an interior that is operating from disorder rather than design.

This is not a statement of condemnation. It is a statement of condition. You did not choose the disordered architecture you inherited. You were born into it. And the patterns it produces — the fear, the striving, the shame, the distance from God that returns no matter how many times you close it on a Sunday — are not character flaws. They are structural symptoms. Evidence of an inner architecture that has not yet been fully restored.

The shame that makes you hide your true self from God and others. The fear that makes His presence feel like an examination rather than a welcome. The blame that deflects accountability in your closest relationships. The exhaustion of working the ground from a soul that is running on empty. These are the inheritance of Eden's fall. All of them are structural. All of them are addressable.

But none of them can be addressed until they are seen clearly. And most people have spent years trying to address the symptoms without ever understanding the source.

Conviction is common. Consistency is rare.

The story does not end in the garden. God clothed Adam and Eve before He sent them out. That was not a small gesture. It was a declaration. Disorder had entered the human story — but God's commitment to restoring order had not ended. It had, in a sense, just begun. The covering He provided in Eden was the first movement in a long story of restoration — a story that runs through every book of Scripture, through the life and death and resurrection of Christ, and into the life of every believer who has ever stood in the gap between who they are on Sunday and who they are on Monday.

God has always been in the business of restoring what disorder broke.

He is not surprised by your patterns. He is not frustrated by your cycles. He is not waiting for you to achieve a level of consistency before He begins His work in you. He is already working. He was working before you recognized the gap. He was working before you had language for what you were experiencing.

He is working now.

We now understand the architecture God built and the moment it was reversed. But knowing what broke and how it broke is only part of the picture. Because disorder, once it enters the interior, does not stay at the level of a single catastrophic event. It moves differently than that. More quietly. More gradually. In ways that most people never recognize until the distance has already become significant.

That is what the next chapter examines.

Not a crisis. A current.

Part Two

The Human Heart After the Fall

IV

The Drift of Everyday Life

*"We must pay closer attention to what we have heard, lest we drift away
from it." — Hebrews 2:1*

On the fourth day, God set the governing lights.

Not to decorate the sky. To govern the day. To rule the night. To serve as
signs for seasons, for days, for years. To give every living thing a way of
knowing where it is, what time it is, and which direction leads home.
The sun and moon were not ornamental. They were navigational.
Without them, nothing in the created order could orient itself. Nothing
could know when to plant or when to rest, when to move or when to
hold still. The governing lights were what made sustained, directional life
possible.

God understood that life without governance cannot endure. It drifts.

The same is true of the interior life. God did not design the human soul
to navigate by feeling alone, or by the urgency of whatever demand

presented itself most loudly on a given Tuesday. He set governing lights in the interior — the spirit's connection to Him, the Word that orients the soul, the Sabbath rhythm that forces the question of what is first. These were not disciplines to be maintained. They were navigational anchors. Orienting forces. The interior equivalent of the sun and moon — designed to tell the soul where it is, what time it is, and which direction leads home.

When those governing lights dim — not through rebellion, but through the gradual accumulation of inattention — the soul does not immediately notice. The horizon looks the same. The water looks the same. Life continues at its ordinary pace. But without the governing orientation, the current begins to carry what is no longer anchored. And drift, unlike collapse, announces nothing. It simply continues.

This chapter is about that drift. What it looks like. How it accumulates. What does it cost? And why the person living in it is often the last to know.

Nobody plans to drift.

That is what makes it so effective.

Drift does not announce itself. There is no moment of decision, no clear turning point where a person chooses distance over alignment. It accumulates instead, in the space between intentions and the ordinary demands of the day. A prayer was skipped because the morning ran late. A Sunday was missed because the week had been exhausting. A conviction quietly set aside because acting on it would have required a difficult conversation.

None of those moments feels significant on its own.

That is the nature of drift. Each movement away from alignment is small enough to seem inconsequential. It is only when you look up — weeks or months later — that you realize how far the current has carried you.

The writer of Hebrews named this danger with unusual precision: "we must pay closer attention to what we have heard, lest we drift away." The word translated as "drift" is a nautical term. It describes a ship that has slipped its anchor. Not a ship that chose to leave port. A ship that was not held securely enough in place — and was gradually carried away by forces it wasn't actively resisting.

That image is exact.

Drift is not rebellion with momentum. It is alignment without an anchor.

I want to tell you about a man I'll call Raymond.

Raymond had been a believer for most of his adult life. He was not dramatic about his faith — he was the steady kind. The man who showed up, who followed through, who could be counted on. His relationship with God had never been characterized by highs and lows so much as by a consistent, quiet presence that had shaped the way he moved through his days.

But over the course of about two years, something had changed. And he could not tell me when it happened.

It had not started with a crisis. There was no betrayal, no catastrophic loss, no single moment where everything tilted. It started with a season of being genuinely, legitimately busy. A promotion at work that came with responsibilities that expanded to fill every available hour. A child entering high school with a schedule that requires near-constant logistical attention. A church community he was still technically part of but increasingly present in only in the most surface way — showing up, greeting the same people, leaving quickly because the week's demands were already reassembling by Sunday afternoon.

He told me, "I didn't stop praying. I just stopped expecting anything when I did."

That sentence stayed with me. Because it names something precise about what gradual disconnection produces in the interior, it is not an absence. It is presence without expectation. The form was maintained, but emptied of the aliveness that once gave it meaning. He was still going through the motions — and he knew they were motions now, which was its own particular kind of grief.

His wife had noticed before he had. She told him he seemed "far away" even when he was physically present. Those conversations that used to go somewhere now stayed at the surface. That she couldn't tell anymore what was happening inside him because he didn't seem to know either, he had not become cold toward her. He had become... absent. Sitting in the room, but not quite in it. Available but not reachable.

He dismissed it at first as stress. As the natural fatigue of a demanding season. As something that would correct itself once the workload eased. But the workload eased, and the absence remained.

Because the absence was not about the workload, the workload had been the occasion for the drift. But the drift had settled into something structural — a gradual severance from the interior anchor that had once kept him connected to God, to his family, and to himself. And once that anchor had quietly slipped, no reduction in external pressure was going to restore what the slipping had taken.

He had not decided to become unreachable. He had stopped being held in place. The governing lights had dimmed. And without them, the current had carried him somewhere he did not choose and could not, on his own, name.

Drift rarely feels like rebellion.

It feels like a distraction.

Life becomes full. Responsibilities accumulate. The schedule that once had a margin no longer does. The quiet morning that created space for God gets absorbed by everything else that needs attention before the day begins. Nothing is rejected. Nothing is renounced. It is crowded out, gradually, by the sheer volume of ordinary life.

Mark recorded Jesus describing this exact process. In the parable of the Sower, He described seed that fell among thorns and initially grew — but was ultimately choked out. The explanation He offered was precise: "The cares of the world and the deceitfulness of riches and the desires for other things enter in and choke the word, and it proves unfruitful."

Cares. Riches. Desires for other things.

Not persecution. Not temptation. Not dramatic spiritual failure. Ordinary life, in sufficient quantity, choked what was once growing.

Drift rarely feels like rebellion. It feels like a distraction.

This is the mechanism most believers never see clearly, because none of the individual elements feels dangerous. The care is legitimate. Responsibility is real. The desire is not inherently wrong. But together, accumulating over time, they create an environment in which alignment cannot sustain itself without intentional resistance.

And most people are not resisting. They are simply living.

Drift is what happens when living becomes the whole project.

Raymond was not a careless man. He was not indifferent to God or to the people in his life. He was living at full capacity in every direction, and the thing that gradually lost its place in the full schedule was the interior work — the reflection, the stillness, the unhurried communion — that alone keeps the anchor in place. Not because he decided that interior work was unimportant. Because it kept getting displaced by urgent things, and urgency, over time, had become the governing principle of how his days were structured.

The cares of the world do not need to be worldly to choke the word. There needs to be many.

Luke recorded a scene in the home of Mary and Martha that has often been read as a lesson about priorities. But it is more accurately a portrait of drift in real time.

Jesus had come to their home. Mary sat at His feet and listened. Martha was "distracted with much serving."

The word Luke used for distracted means to be pulled away and drawn in a different direction by competing demands. Martha was not indifferent to Jesus. She was not hostile to what Mary was receiving. She was overwhelmed by the legitimate work of hospitality — work that was, in itself, an act of care and honor.

But the urgent crowded out the essentials.

When Martha finally surfaced from the pressure long enough to speak, she didn't say she had lost interest in Jesus. She said she was distracted and pulled in too many directions. Carrying more than she could hold while simultaneously trying to be present to what actually mattered.

Jesus' response is one of the most tender diagnoses in the Gospels:

"Martha, Martha, you are anxious and troubled about many things, but one thing is necessary."

Anxious and troubled about many things.

Not rebellious. Not faithless. Anxious. Scattered across too many legitimate concerns to remain anchored to the one that ordered everything else. The governing light had not been extinguished. It had been obscured by the press of everything she was trying to manage.

No one wakes up planning to drift from God. It happens slowly.

That is the portrait of drift. Not a person who chose distance. A person whose attention was consumed by so many real and pressing things that the one thing necessary kept getting displaced.

And over time, displacement becomes distance.

Raymond recognized himself in this picture immediately. He had not chosen to drift any more than Martha had chosen to miss what was happening in her own living room. He had chosen, thousands of times, to handle the next pressing thing. Each choice was reasonable. Together, they had produced a life in which the one thing necessary had been displaced so consistently and for so long that he had forgotten what it felt like when it was not.

Drift is not only a spiritual condition. It is an interior one.

When alignment begins to slip, the first casualty is not belief. It is the quality of a person's inner life in the ordinary hours. The texture of how Monday morning actually feels. The ambient state of the soul as it moves through an unremarkable Tuesday afternoon.

In the early stages of drift, most people still have their theology intact. They still believe the same things. They still attend the same services.

They still pray, at least occasionally, with some measure of expectation. But something in the interior has begun to flatten. The richness that once characterized their awareness of God in the ordinary moments grows thin. The capacity to sense His presence in a commute, a conversation, a quiet moment before sleep — that capacity quietly diminishes.

The soul that is drifting is not a soul in crisis. It is a soul that is simply operating at a lower register than it was designed for. Not in collapse, but not fully alive. Managing rather than abiding. Coping rather than drawing from the vine. Surviving the week rather than inhabiting it.

This lower register becomes the new normal so gradually that most people cannot identify precisely when the shift happened. They only know that something that once felt natural now feels like effort. Prayer that once felt like a conversation now feels like an obligation. Worship that once felt like genuinely coming home now has the quality of performing an activity they know matters, but cannot feel in the way they once did.

And because the drift has been gradual, they attribute the flatness to something else entirely. A difficult season. Spiritual dryness that comes and goes. Getting older. The natural ebb and flow of faith.

Very few identify it correctly as drift, as the accumulated consequence of an anchor that has been slowly loosening for months or years.

---

*The drifting soul is not in crisis. It is operating below
the register for which it was designed.*

Raymond had arrived at a working theory for his flatness: he was simply a different kind of person than he had been in his twenties. More pragmatic. Less given to the kind of interior intensity that had characterized his earlier faith. He had decided, without ever quite deciding, that what he was experiencing was maturity rather than loss. That the quieter, flatter version of his interior life was simply what adult faith looked like.

It was not. It was a drift that had lasted long enough to be mistaken for temperament.

And that misidentification was the most dangerous thing about it — because a person who has concluded that their drift is simply who they are has no reason to look for what has slipped. They have stopped checking the anchor's position. They have accepted the current condition as permanent.
Drift does not stay contained to the interior. It surfaces in the places where the interior expresses itself.

In work, the drifting soul loses access to something difficult to name but unmistakable when it is gone. A quality of engagement. The capacity to bring something more than competence to what they do. Work that flows from an aligned interior carries a steadiness under pressure, a generosity toward the people in the room, an absence of the low-grade anxiety that turns ordinary work stress into something that feels existentially threatening.

When drift takes hold, work becomes heavier. Not because the actual workload has necessarily changed, but because the interior doing the work has less to draw from. The person brings more effort to the same tasks and receives less satisfaction from them. The gap between Sunday's clarity and Monday's reality feels widest in these moments — in the middle of a workday, under ordinary pressure, when the distance between who they are at church and who they are at the desk feels impossible to cross.

In relationships, drift manifests as a slow withdrawal of presence. Not deliberate withdrawal — the drifting person does not decide to become less available to the people they love. But the interior, which has grown thin, lacks the reserves to give what real presence requires. Listening to that is genuinely attentive. Patience does not require effort. The kind of care that is not depleted by stress or contingent on the other person doing their part.

These capacities come from a soul drawing on a deep source. When that source connection weakens, the capacities diminish with it. The relationships most affected are the closest. The spouse who notices a quality of distraction that was not there before. The child who senses that the parent is physically present but not quite there. The friend who finds that conversations with depth have become pleasant but surface-level.

Small misalignments, repeated daily, eventually create large distances.

Raymond's wife had been reading the drift accurately for months before he acknowledged it; what she experienced as his absence was not a character failure on his part. It was the expression of a relational interior that had lost its governing orientation. He genuinely wanted to be present to her. He genuinely wanted to be the father his children needed. But the soul that had once generated that presence from overflow was now running from empty, and empty cannot give what presence requires, no matter how sincere the intention.

There is a specific place where drift becomes most visible to the person experiencing it, though they rarely recognize what they are seeing.

Scripture stops landing.

Not in any dramatic sense. The words are still familiar. The passages that once moved deep within are still recognizable as true. But the aliveness is gone. The drifting person can read a verse that once broke them open and feel almost nothing. They can sit through a well-preached sermon and find their minds wandering before the first point is finished. They can open their Bible with genuine intention and find the page going flat.

This experience produces its own particular kind of discouragement. Because if God's word is living and active, as Hebrews 4 promises, then the absence of that aliveness feels like evidence of something wrong with the reader. They wonder if they have lost their faith. They wonder if they were ever as close to God as they thought they were.

None of those conclusions is accurate.

The word has not gone flat. The reader has drifted to a place where they cannot currently receive it. The interior that was once oriented toward God — open, attentive, expectant — has become crowded, defended, and preoccupied. The same signal is being broadcast. The antenna has been repositioned.

Think about what Day 4 was actually for. The governing lights were set so that living things could orient themselves — could know when to receive, when to rest, when to move. Scripture functions the same way in the interior life. It is not primarily information. It is orientation. It tells the soul where it is, what is true, and which direction leads back to the source. But an interior that is no longer looking up at the governing light cannot receive the orientation it is being offered.

Raymond had stopped reading his Bible, not because he decided it was unimportant but because it had stopped doing anything. He had sat with it enough times in that flat, unreceiving state that the practice had begun to feel like confirmation of the distance rather than a path out of it. Every morning that the page stayed flat felt like further evidence that the God who had once spoken through those pages was no longer available to him in that way.

He had not rejected the word. He had run out of the interior conditions required to receive it. And no one had told him that those conditions were addressable. That which had slipped could be restored. That the flatness was not the final word on his relationship with God — it was a navigational indicator pointing toward the structural work that alone could reverse it.

Drift also changes the way a person makes decisions — and most people never connect the two.

When the interior is aligned, decisions flow from a settled center. Not every decision is easy, but there is a governing orientation beneath them — a sense of what matters most, a clarity about values and direction that makes the hard choices legible even when they are not comfortable. The person does not need to reconstruct their identity from scratch every time a significant choice appears. They are deciding from somewhere. They know who they are and what they are for, and those anchors shape the decisions before the deliberation begins.

This is what Day 4 was actually providing. The sun and moon did not make decisions for the created order. They gave the created order the orientation that enabled the right decisions. Plants knew when to grow. Animals knew when to move. Seasons turned into their proper sequence. The governing lights did not make the living — they made the living directional.

When drift has taken hold of the interior, that settled center gradually erodes. Decisions that once felt straightforward begin to feel complicated. Not because the external circumstances have necessarily changed, but because the internal reference point has shifted. The drifting person finds themselves deliberating longer, second-guessing more, and arriving at decisions with less confidence than they once did.

Over time, this produces a pattern of avoidance. The drifting person begins to delay decisions they would once have made quickly. They defer to others on questions they would once have led. They choose the familiar over the faithful, not because the familiar is better, but because the faithful requires a clarity they can no longer reliably access.

What the drifting person interprets as indecisiveness or fear is usually something simpler: they have lost access to the governing orientation that made clear decisions possible. The problem is not that they cannot decide. The problem is that they are deciding without the anchor that decision-making requires.

Drift does not just affect how a person feels. It changes how they function.

Drift operates through accumulation, not through decision.

It begins with fragmented attention. The mind that once had space to stay anchored to what matters most becomes crowded with competing inputs. Not because those inputs are evil — most of them are not — but because the soul was not designed to carry an unlimited number of concerns simultaneously without losing its center.

When attention fragments, reflection disappears. And reflection is the mechanism through which conviction stays alive. It is the practice of regularly returning to the things that orient the inner life. Without it, truth does not deepen — it fades. Not through rejection, but through neglect. The same way a language you once spoke fluently grows distant when you stop using it.

When reflection disappears, urgency moves in to fill the space. Urgency is not inherently destructive. But a life governed entirely by urgency has no room for the deeper questions that anchor a soul. Where is my life heading? What is actually shaping my decisions? What is the distance between what I believe and how I'm living? These questions require stillness to answer. And urgency is the enemy of stillness.

The soul that lives perpetually in urgency gradually stops asking the questions that would reveal how far it has drifted.

This is the quiet mathematics of drift. No single day is the problem. No single distraction is the turning point. It is the cumulative effect of small displacements, each one unremarkable, that eventually adds up to a life that has moved a significant distance from its intended direction.

The person who experiences this rarely has a clear moment they can point to and say, "That's when it changed." It changed in the space between a hundred ordinary moments. That is what makes it so difficult to address — and so easy to miss until the distance is already significant.

The warning in Hebrews was written to people who had not abandoned their faith. They had stopped paying close attention to it.

The Greek word translated "pay closer attention" means to hold something near. To keep it close. To not let it drift to the periphery of your awareness, where other things can gradually push it further out.

The writer was not warning against dramatic apostasy. He was warning against the slow loosening of the anchor that precedes it. The incremental inattention. The gradual crowding out. The drift that happens not in one moment of decision but in a hundred moments of distraction.

An unanchored ship does not immediately crash. It drifts. Sometimes for a long time. The horizon looks the same. The water looks the same. The drift is only visible when you check your position against something fixed.

The governing lights are that fixed reference. They do not move. The soul's distance from them is always measurable — if the soul is willing to look up long enough to check.

Most people check their position infrequently. Life does not encourage it. The pace of modern existence actively discourages the stillness required to do it honestly. And so the drift continues, quiet and gradual, until the distance from where they started becomes impossible to deny.

Raymond had not checked his position in years. Not because he was afraid of what he would find, but because there had never seemed to be a moment that was still enough. The family. The work. The obligations that kept reassembling the moment one was addressed. He had stayed in motion in part because motion had made it possible not to look at how far the current had carried him.

When he finally stopped — when the stillness became unavoidable, as it eventually does for everyone who has drifted long enough — the distance surprised him. Not because it was catastrophic. Because it was so ordinary. He had not gone anywhere dramatic. He had ended up, through a thousand unremarkable displacements, in a place that felt nothing like home.

Over time, drift produces a recognizable pattern.

It begins with episodic clarity. Moments — in worship, in prayer, in a conversation that breaks something open — when the distance collapses and alignment briefly returns. The soul surfaces from the drift and remembers what it feels like to be anchored. The conviction is real. The desire to stay there is genuine.

Then the week returns.

The demands reassemble. The urgency resumes. And without the structural support to hold what the moment of clarity produced, the soul gradually drifts back to where it was. Not through any conscious choice. Simply because the current is stronger than the anchor.

This cycle — clarity, drift, clarity, drift — becomes so familiar that many believers stop questioning it. They begin to assume it is simply the normal rhythm of faith. The spiritual high that fades. The conviction that weakens. The recommitment that doesn't hold.

They normalize the gap.

And in normalizing it, they stop looking for what would actually close it.

The greatest spiritual danger is not collapse. It is a gradual drift.

This matters because, left unaddressed, drift does not stabilize. It accelerates. The soul that has drifted for years develops patterns of perception and response that become increasingly resistant to the moments of clarity that might otherwise interrupt them. The distance between Sunday and Monday widens. The gap between what is believed and what is lived grows. And the person carrying all of it begins, slowly, to accept it as the permanent condition of their life.

That acceptance is the most dangerous place drift can deliver you.

Not because God has given up. He hasn't.

But because the soul has stopped expecting anything different.
There is one more consequence of extended drift that is rarely named but deeply significant.

It changes how a person sees God.

Not their theological statements about God — those often remain intact for years after the drift has settled in. The drifting person can still articulate correct doctrine. They can still affirm the right things in conversation. But the lived, experiential image of God — the God they actually encounter in the interior moments of their ordinary days — quietly shifts.

The God of the aligned interior is a God of nearness. A God who is present in the commute and the conversation and the difficulty and the quiet moment before sleep. A God whose presence is not reserved for Sundays or crisis moments but is woven through the fabric of an ordinary life that has been structured around His governance. The person who lives in this alignment does not think about God constantly in a forced or artificial way. They move through their days with a settled awareness of being held, of being known, of operating within a life that has an Author and a direction.

The God of the drifting interior is a God of distance. Not theologically distant — the person still believes God is omnipresent, still affirms His faithfulness. But experientially distant. A God who feels most available in the elevated moments and most absent in the ordinary ones. A God who seems to show up in the sermon but not in the staff meeting. A

God who was real during the retreat but hard to locate on the drive home.

This is perhaps the most costly consequence of long-term drift. Not the missed quiet times or the weakened disciplines or the reduced engagement with Scripture. But the slow erosion of the lived sense that God is present in all of it — that the ordinary hours of an ordinary day are the very territory in which He is most interested in being known.

Raymond described this to me in a way that I have not forgotten. He said, "I still believe God is everywhere. I don't experience Him anywhere."

That sentence is one of the most honest descriptions of advanced drift I have ever heard. The theology intact. The experience hollowed out. The conviction is present. The felt sense of being accompanied — of moving through an authored life rather than an accidental one — gone so gradually that by the time he noticed its absence, he could not remember exactly what it had felt like when it was there.

Most people who recognize the drift in their lives respond by trying to recover.

Recovery is a return to a previous state. It means getting back to where you were before the drift began. Back to the discipline. Back to the consistency. Back to the spiritual practices that marked an earlier, healthier season. Recovery is the most natural response to drift because it is oriented toward something familiar — a version of the person's life that actually felt aligned, that they can remember and reach for.

The problem with recovery is that it sets the ceiling at the starting point of the drift. It aims to return to where the anchor slipped, without asking why the anchor slipped in the first place. And if the structural conditions that produced the original drift have not changed — if the interior has not been rebuilt in a way that addresses the root rather than the symptoms, then recovery typically produces exactly what it has produced every time before: a period of improved consistency followed by the gradual resumption of the same drift.

Recovery and restoration are not the same thing.

Restoration goes deeper than recovery. It does not aim to return the person to a previous state. It aims to rebuild the interior on a more secure foundation than the one that existed before the drift began—not getting back to where you were, but being rebuilt into something more structurally sound than what existed before.

This is the difference between trying harder and being changed. Recovery requires effort. Restoration requires surrender. Recovery is something you do. Restoration is something God does in you — as you make yourself available to the rebuilding rather than simply reaching back for the spiritual rhythms that will once again, on their own, prove insufficient to hold what is needed.

The person who has been through the drift-recovery-drift cycle has evidence that recovery is not the answer. That evidence is not discouraging. It is clarifying. It is pointing them past recovery toward the deeper work that drift was always an invitation to begin.

Raymond eventually understood this distinction. He had tried recovery four times in two years. Each attempt had produced real improvement for a period of weeks, sometimes months. And then the same drift had reasserted itself — not dramatically, not through any single failure, just through the same quiet displacement of the same priorities by the same pressures until he stopped reaching for the previous version of his spiritual life and started asking what it would mean to build something more structurally sound than what had slipped.

That question was the beginning of something genuinely different.

If you have recognized yourself in this chapter, it is worth pausing on what that recognition actually means.

It does not mean you are failing. It means you are human, living east of Eden, in a world that is actively inhospitable to the alignment your soul was designed for. Drift is not a character flaw. It is the predictable result of an interior operating in an environment that accelerates disorder rather than healing it.

But recognition is the beginning of something.

Because drift continues most effectively in the dark — in the space where the pattern has not yet been named, where the gap has not yet been measured, where the distance has not yet been honestly assessed, the moment you can see it clearly, something shifts. Not the drift itself, not yet. But your relationship to it.

You stop assuming it is inevitable.

And that is the first movement toward something different.

But there is still something that needs to be understood before the rebuilding can begin. We have seen the architecture God designed. We have seen the moment disorder entered and reversed that sequence. We have seen how drift carries the soul further and further from its governing orientation across ordinary days.

What we have not yet answered is this: why does the clarity that arrives in the good moments — in worship, in prayer, in the genuine encounters that Sunday keeps producing — why does it keep failing to hold?

On Day 5, God filled the prepared spaces with life. Birds filled the sky. Fish filled the sea. Life went where the structure had been built to receive it.

But if the governing lights of Day 4 are not in place, the life that arrives has no orientation. It cannot find its space. It cannot stay where it lands.

That is exactly why clarity fades.

And that is where the next chapter begins.

V

Why Clarity Fades

"Anyone who listens to the word but does not do what it says is like someone who looks at his face in a mirror and, after looking at himself, goes away and immediately forgets what he looks like." — James 1:23–24

On the fifth day, God filled the prepared spaces.

The sky that had been structured and separated and governed by light — He filled it with birds. The seas that had been gathered and bounded and ordered — He filled them with fish. Life went exactly where the structure had been built to receive it. Not randomly. Not indiscriminately. Each living thing found its prepared space and flourished there, because the conditions that made flourishing possible had been established in the days before it arrived.

The fish do not swim in the sky. The birds do not live in the sea. Life holds where it was designed to hold — and only where the structure beneath it was prepared to receive it.

This is the principle that explains one of the most frustrating experiences in the life of faith.

Clarity keeps arriving. Sunday keeps producing genuine moments of spiritual life — real encounters, real conviction, real movement in the interior. The bird is real. The fish is real. The life that lands in the moment of worship is not manufactured or imagined. But by Wednesday, it is gone. Not because it was false. Because it landed in a space that had not been prepared to receive and hold it. The interior structure — fractured by the fall, reversed in its sequence, further disordered by years of drift — cannot do for clarity what the sea does for the fish. It cannot provide the conditions for a sustainable life.

The problem is not that clarity doesn't come. It comes consistently, faithfully, with every Sunday and every genuine moment of encounter. The problem is that the interior has not yet been prepared to hold what keeps arriving.

This chapter explains why. And why understanding it changes everything about what the solution looks like.

Clarity arrives.

That is not the problem.

Most believers have experienced genuine moments of spiritual clarity. A sermon that named exactly what was broken. A verse that arrived at precisely the right moment and landed with unmistakable weight. A season of prayer that produced a sense of direction so certain it felt like the ground had stabilized beneath them.

The clarity was real. The experience was not manufactured or imagined.

But then it faded.

Not immediately. Not through any conscious rejection. It simply lost its hold over the days that followed, quietly retreating as the ordinary demands of life reassembled around it. And the person who received it was left trying to understand why something that felt so undeniable could become so distant so quickly.

This is the question this chapter answers.

Not why clarity doesn't come — it does. But why doesn't it stay?

I want to tell you about a man I'll call Thomas.

Thomas was the kind of person who genuinely loved the things of God. He was not performing that love. He was not wearing it as a social identity. He read widely, thought carefully, and asked real questions. He took his faith seriously in the way people who have encountered something true do — not out of obligation, but out of recognition.

But there was a problem Thomas had been living with for years without ever quite naming it.

Every time genuine clarity arrived — and it arrived regularly, because Thomas was the kind of person who put himself in the path of it — it would stay with him for a day, sometimes two, before the week began to erode it. He could trace the arc precisely: the Sunday moment, the Monday morning where it was still present but competing with the inbox, the Wednesday where it had receded to background, the Friday where it felt like something he'd read about rather than something he'd experienced.

What made Thomas's situation particular was that his life was genuinely full. Not full in the undisciplined sense — he was organized, productive, capable. Full in the way that the life of a serious, responsible man in his late thirties tends to be full: a demanding career, a marriage that required real investment, children at the age where they needed his presence, not just his provision, a church community he was genuinely engaged with, and friendships he tried to maintain. Every one of those things was good. None of them was optional. All of them together had produced a life in which the interior work — the unhurried reception, the sustained reflection, the stillness required to let clarity take root — kept getting displaced by things that were not only urgent but genuinely important.

He told me, "I don't waste time. I don't have any left over for the things that would actually make the time I have worth something."

That sentence is worth sitting with. He was not talking about productivity. He was talking about the interior conditions required to steward what clarity delivers. And he had correctly identified that those conditions had been crowded out — not by carelessness, not by sin, but by the sheer volume of legitimate demands that had filled every available margin of his life.

The signal was arriving. The noise was simply louder.

Thomas would come home from a Sunday service where something real had happened in his interior. By Sunday evening, the week was already reassembling: the email that needed a response before Monday, the child's project that needed attention, the conversation with his wife that had been deferred from Thursday. None of those things was wrong. All of them together meant that the clarity he had received that morning had no quiet space to settle into. It was received into a life running at full volume, and a life running at full volume cannot hold what requires stillness to take root.

He described it as feeling permanently behind. Not behind on tasks — he kept up with those, behind himself. Behind on the interior work that he knew mattered and kept failing to find a way to prioritize because everything else that mattered was already filling the space where that work needed to happen.

The enemy had not needed to tempt Thomas away from his faith. He had needed to ensure that Thomas's life stayed full enough that the signal God was consistently sending could never quite break through the noise long enough to take root. Not a dramatic strategy. A patient one. And it had been working for years.

James chose an image so precise that it is almost uncomfortable.

He described a person who looks at their face in a mirror, then walks away and immediately forgets what they look like.

The image's strangeness is the point. No one actually does that with a physical mirror. You look, you see something real, and that perception stays with you. You carry it with you when you leave.

But James was describing something that happens constantly with spiritual clarity.

A person receives truth. They look directly at it. They see something real about themselves, about God, about the direction their life needs to move. And then they walk away — back into the day, back into the routine, back into the pace of ordinary life — and the image fades. Not because the truth changed. Because nothing in their structure was built to hold it.

The mirror showed them something true.

The moment they looked away, it was gone.

Think about this, considering Day 5. When God filled the sea with fish, the sea was prepared to receive them. The fish didn't land on dry ground and wondered why they couldn't stay. The structure had been built to hold the life that arrived. The mirror-gazer's problem is precisely the Day 5 problem in reverse — life keeps arriving, but the prepared space is absent. The interior that receives the moment of clarity is not yet structured to sustain it. The fish lands on dry ground.

Clarity without structure cannot sustain itself.

James is not describing a failure of sincerity. The person looked. They engaged with what they saw. The problem is not that they refused to see it; it is that seeing alone produced no lasting change in how they moved through the world.

Insight without architecture is decoration.

It brightens a moment. It does not rebuild a life.

For Thomas, the mirror image was especially precise. He was a man who looked often. He engaged with the truth regularly and seriously. His problem was not that he refused to look at what the mirror showed him. His problem was that the moment he turned away from the mirror, the ten other things waiting in the hallway immediately occupied his full attention, and the image — however real, however significant — had no protected space in his interior where it could remain visible until he was ready to build on it.

The fading, in his case, was not the result of insincerity. It was the predictable result of a life structured in a way that left no room for what clarity requires after it arrives.

It is worth being specific about what the fading actually feels like from the inside, because the person experiencing it rarely has language for it.

In the first hours after a moment of genuine clarity, everything feels different. The interior is quieter. The direction feels obvious. The thing that needed to change seems entirely within reach. The person leaves the service, or closes the Bible, or ends the prayer with a quality of settledness they have not felt in weeks. Something really happened. Something shifted.

By evening, the settledness is still mostly present, though the edges have softened slightly. The demands of the afternoon have accumulated in the margins. The clarity is still there, but it is no longer the only thing in the room.

By the next morning, the day begins with its ordinary requirements. The inbox. The responsibilities. The conversations that need to happen. The clarity is accessible if the person reaches for it, but it is no longer the automatic foreground of their awareness. It has receded into the background.

By midweek, it has the quality of a memory rather than a present reality. The person can recall what they felt. They can restate what they received. But the living force of it — the weight that made it feel undeniable — has diminished to the point where it no longer moves decisions. It has become information rather than conviction.

By the following Sunday, the cycle is ready to begin again.

This is not dramatic. That is exactly the point. The fading is so gradual, so unremarkable at each stage, that most people do not notice it happening until they are already on the far side of it. They do not experience a moment of losing clarity. They eventually experience that it is gone.

Thomas had lived with this arc so many times that he could narrate it from memory. He knew by Sunday afternoon roughly when the clarity would begin to feel thin. He had stopped being surprised by the fade. He had begun to expect it, which was in some ways more costly than the fading itself — because expectation shapes reception. A person who arrives at Sunday's clarity already half-anticipating Friday's fade is not receiving the clarity with the full openness it deserves. They are receiving it with a defensive posture formed by too many prior cycles.

---

*Most believers experience spiritual clarity. Few build
lives that can hold it.*

Jesus told a story about two builders that most people have heard so
many times that it no longer lands with its original force.

Two men. Two houses. One built on rock; one built on sand. A storm
arrives—one household. One collapses.

The detail most people miss is this: both houses looked identical before
the storm.

From the outside, during calm weather, there was no visible difference
between the man who built on rock and the man who built on sand.
Both had a structure. Both appeared stable. Both were functional in
ordinary conditions.

The storm did not create a weakness in the house built on sand. It
revealed one that was already there.

Jesus was not telling a story about dramatic spiritual failure. He was
describing the invisible difference between two lives that appear similar
on the surface — both exposed to the same truth, both responsive to it
in the moment — but are built on fundamentally different foundations.

The man who built on rock heard the same words—received the same
clarity. But he did something with it that the other man did not. He
built. He took what he received and let it restructure something beneath

the surface of his life — something that would hold when the conditions changed.

The man who built on sand received the clarity, too. But the clarity remained at the surface. It was informed without restructuring. It inspired without rebuilding.

When the storm came, the difference became visible.

The storm is not always dramatic. Sometimes it is simply Monday.

Thomas recognized himself in the second builder immediately. Not because he was careless — he was not. But because the clarity he had been receiving for years had remained, repeatedly, at the surface. He had heard it. He had been genuinely moved by it. He had formed genuine intentions based on it. But the building — the slow, patient, structural work of letting what he received actually reshape the interior beneath the surface — had never happened. Not because he refused. Because he had never understood that it was a separate step, distinct from the receiving itself, and one that required something his life had not been structured to provide.

The question worth pressing on is why clarity so consistently fails to produce the structure that would hold it.

Part of the answer is environmental. The world east of Eden is not neutral toward alignment. It is actively inhospitable to it. The pace, the noise, the relentless accumulation of demands — these are not simply inconveniences. They are conditions that erode the structure unless it is intentionally maintained. Clarity received in a protected moment must survive contact with an environment that was not designed to sustain it.

Think about what happens in the hours immediately following a genuine moment of spiritual clarity. The service ends. The conversation closes. The prayer time concludes. And the person steps back into the full current of their ordinary life: the phone notifications that accumulated, the decision that needs to be made before the end of the day, the relationship tension that hasn't been resolved, the financial pressure that was present before the moment of clarity and is still present after it.

Clarity does not come with a protected environment. It arrives at the existing one.

And the existing environment built over the years around urgency, demand, and the full volume of ordinary life — does not pause to make room for what the clarity is trying to accomplish. It simply continues. And the clarity, which has no structural home to return to in the interior, begins almost immediately to lose ground against the current.

This is not a failure of the moment. It is a mismatch between what the moment produces and what the interior is prepared to receive and retain.

---

*Truth received in a moment must be housed in a
structure that outlasts the moment.*

The deeper answer is interior.

The soul that receives clarity is the same soul that carries the architectural disorder inherited from the fall. And a disordered interior cannot automatically translate what the spirit receives into durable structural change. The insight lands. The emotion responds—the intention forms. But the soul, still operating from its reversed sequence, does not know how to build on what it just received.

It experiences clarity. It cannot be constructed with it.

This is why two people can sit in the same service, receive the same truth, feel equally moved, and walk out into completely different trajectories. One carries the moment as an inspiration that gradually fades. The other carries it as a stone that becomes part of something being built. The difference is not the quality of their faith. It is the condition of the interior structure receiving it.

Thomas had sat next to men whose clarity seemed to hold in a way his did not. He had attributed the difference to personality, to temperament, to the kind of natural spiritual gravitas some people seem to have, and others do not. It had not occurred to him that what he was observing was a structural difference — not a gifting gap, not a discipline gap, not a faith gap, but an architectural one. And architectural differences, unlike personality differences, are addressable.

Paul described in Galatians a conflict that operates directly beneath the surface of spiritual experience:

"For the flesh desires what is contrary to the Spirit, and the Spirit what is contrary to the flesh. They are in conflict with each other, so that you are not to do whatever you want."

The conflict Paul describes does not pause when clarity arrives. It is present in the moment of clarity and in every moment after it. The Spirit receives truth and moves toward it. The flesh — the soul and body still operating from the disordered sequence introduced by the fall — pulls in a different direction.

This means that every moment of genuine clarity is immediately contested.

Not by an external enemy. By the internal architecture of a soul that has not yet been fully restored to order. The clarity is real. The pull away from it is also real. And without a structure that holds clarity in place while the soul is being rebuilt around it, the contest is unequal.

The flesh has momentum. History. Established patterns. Grooves worn deep by years of habitual response. When pressure arrives, the interior does not reach the clarity received last Sunday. It reaches for what it has always done. The familiar. The practice. The path of least resistance that the disordered soul has been walking for years.

Clarity has truth. But truth without structure cannot hold against momentum.

Thomas understood this dynamic viscerally once it was named. Clarity was never the problem. The week after the clarity was the problem. The moment when the full weight of his ordinary life reassembled and the interior, rather than reaching for what Sunday had delivered, reached instead for its established patterns — the efficiency, the productivity, the forward motion that had served him well professionally but had never been ordered around anything deeper than the next urgent thing.

He was not a man lacking spiritual desire. He was a man whose interior momentum ran in a direction that clarity kept interrupting but could not redirect, because redirection requires a structure the interruption alone cannot build.

It is worth slowing down to describe what this conflict actually feels like from the inside, because most people experience it without recognizing it.

The clarity arrives on Sunday with genuine force. The interior is moved. Something shifts in the spirit. An intention forms — to address that relationship, to reorder that priority, to stop carrying that particular fear, and actually give it to God. The intention is sincere. In that moment, it feels like something has genuinely changed.

Monday arrives. The clarity is still nominally present — the person remembers having it. But it has lost the emotional force it carried the day before. The relationship that needed to be addressed is still complicated, and the complications feel more immediate than the clarity. The priority that needs reordering requires disrupting systems that work, even if they work at the cost of alignment. The fear that needed to be released is still there, and releasing it requires trusting God with something that feels genuinely dangerous to let go of.

So the person defers. Not consciously. Not with the internal language of rejection. They move through Monday doing what Monday requires, and the clarity recedes to the background where it will wait, increasingly quiet, until the next moment of genuine spiritual engagement recalls it briefly to the surface.

This is the flesh-spirit conflict in its most ordinary form. Not dramatic temptation. Not a crisis of faith. Just the steady gravitational pull of the established interior toward what it has always done, gently but persistently overcoming the intention that had nowhere permanent to land.

For Thomas, this was Monday by 9 AM. The inbox was open. The first meeting was at ten. The child needed something before school that took 20 minutes, which he hadn't budgeted for. By the time he sat down at his desk, the interior that had been moved on Sunday was already operating in a mode that Sunday's clarity had not been given any structural purchase to interrupt. Not because he chose to leave it behind. Because the life he was walking back into had never been structured to receive it.

The soul does not need more clarity. It needs the
structure to hold what it already has.

After enough cycles of this, the fading begins to produce something more damaging than disappointment.

It produces a conclusion.

The person who has received genuine clarity and watched it fade — not once, not twice, but repeatedly over months and years — eventually arrives at a quiet, rarely spoken belief about themselves. The belief is not usually articulated out loud. It does not typically show up in their public spiritual language. But it shapes everything about how they engage with the next moment of clarity that arrives.

The belief is this: I am not the kind of person who changes.

Not a theological conclusion. Not a statement about God's power or willingness. A personal one, drawn from the accumulated evidence of their own experience. They have felt the clarity. They have made their intentions. They have recommitted more times than they can count. And the pattern has been the same every time. The conviction fades. The behavior returns. The gap between Sunday and Monday reasserts itself like a tide that cannot permanently be held back.

From the inside, this does not feel like giving up. It feels like realism. It feels like the mature acceptance of a person who has learned, through repeated experience, what they can and cannot sustain. They continue to attend. They continue to engage. They continue to believe the right things. But underneath the continued engagement is a settled expectation that nothing will fundamentally change — that the gap is permanent, the cycle is inevitable, and the best available outcome is management rather than transformation.

That expectation is the most costly byproduct of fading. Not because it is true. It is not true. But because it functions as true, it shapes how the person receives the next moment of clarity before it arrives. They receive it already halfway defended against its implications, already anticipating the fade, already quietly preparing for the return of the familiar distance.

The cycle is self-reinforcing. The fading produces a conclusion. The conclusion weakens the reception. The weakened reception accelerates the fading. And the person moves through years of genuine spiritual engagement without the transformation that was always available, held back not by God's unwillingness but by a belief formed in the wreckage of too many cycles that were never understood correctly.

Thomas had arrived at a version of this conclusion. He had not stopped pursuing clarity. But he had quietly stopped expecting it to stick. He came to Sunday with genuine openness, experienced genuine moments, and left with genuine intentions — and somewhere in the background, running beneath all of that sincerity, was the settled knowledge that by Thursday he would be exactly where he had been the Thursday before. Not because he had decided to be. Because he had learned, from years of experience, that that was how his interior worked.

That knowledge was not accurate. It was the misdiagnosis of a structural problem as a personal one. The fade was not a feature of Thomas's character. It was a predictable consequence of clarity arriving in a life whose interior had never been structured to hold it. And structural problems, unlike character problems, have structural solutions.

The greatest barrier to transformation is not lack of desire. It is the conclusion drawn from watching clarity fade too many times.

There is a distinction that clarifies everything about why clarity fades, and it is one the modern church has largely lost.

The distinction is between information and formation.

Information is what the moment of clarity delivers—a truth, a conviction, an insight that accurately names something real. Information is necessary. It is good. It is the raw material of everything that follows. But information alone does not form anything. It describes. It illuminates. It points.

Formation is what happens when information is received into a structure that allows it to reshape the interior over time. Formation is the process by which truth moves from something the person knows to something the person is—from a belief held intellectually to a reality lived structurally. From the surface of the soul to its governing center.

The modern approach to spiritual growth has been heavily weighted toward information. More messages. More content. More truth delivered in more accessible formats to more people more frequently. And information has never been more available than it is now. A person can fill every quiet moment of their day with excellent, accurate, deeply biblical content. And still experience the clarity-fade cycle.

Because information without formation produces a soul that knows more and is changed less, the accumulation of insight without the structural work of receiving and building on it creates a kind of spiritual inflation — where the value of each moment of clarity decreases because there are so many of them. None of them is being given the time and interior space required to actually form something.

Formation is slower than information. It requires stillness that information consumption does not. It requires the willingness to receive one thing deeply rather than many things broadly. And it requires the internal architecture — the ordered interior — that makes deep reception possible in the first place.

The person who is perpetually consuming spiritual content without experiencing lasting change is not lacking information. They are lacking the formation process that would allow the information to do what it was designed to do.

Thomas, to his credit, recognized this instantly. He was not a man who lacked content. His phone had four podcast apps, all curated toward exactly the kind of truth he was genuinely hungry for. He could tell you the argument of every book he had read in the last two years on spiritual formation, leadership, and theology. The information was not the bottleneck. The bottleneck was the interior space — the unhurried, unscheduled, unpressured margin where information becomes formation — that his life had been structured to eliminate.

He was the mirror-gazer James described, turning away from a reflection he had looked at clearly, not because he was careless, but because the hallway outside the mirror was always full.

Paul's instruction in Romans 12 is one of the most quoted and least understood verses in the New Testament.

"Do not conform to the pattern of this world, but be transformed by the renewing of your mind."

Most people read "renewing of your mind" as a reference to thinking better thoughts, replacing negative patterns with positive ones, and choosing to believe the truth rather than lies.

That reading is not wrong. But it is incomplete.

The word translated "transformed" is the Greek word from which we get metamorphosis. It does not describe a surface change. It describes a structural one. The kind of change that happens from the inside out, altering the form of the thing being changed rather than simply its appearance.

A caterpillar does not improve its caterpillar nature through better thinking. It is rebuilt entirely. What emerges is not a better version of what went in. It is a structurally different creature operating from a completely different design.

Paul is not describing a mindset shift. He is describing a rebuilding. And rebuilding takes more than a moment of clarity. It requires clarity to be received, retained, and built upon — repeatedly, over time — until the structure of the inner life has actually changed shape. Until the interior that once reached for the familiar patterns of the disordered soul has been rebuilt into something that reaches instead toward what the spirit has been receiving all along.

Clarity is the beginning of that process.
It is not the process itself.

*Moments of inspiration are powerful. But moments
cannot sustain a life.*

The people who hold clarity are not different categories of believers.

They are not more gifted, more disciplined, or more spiritually exceptional than the people who watch it fade. The difference is not the intensity of their experience in the moment of clarity. Some of the people who hold it most durably receive it quietly, without dramatic emotion, in the margins of an ordinary Tuesday rather than in the heightened atmosphere of Sunday service.

The difference is structural. They have — either through intentional pursuit or through the grace of having been formed in an environment that built it into them — an interior that is ordered well enough to receive what clarity delivers and hold it while it does its work—not perfectly ordered. Not fully restored, but ordered enough that the anchor has something to grip.

This matters because it means the ability to hold clarity is not a personality trait or a spiritual gift that some people have and others do not. It is a structural condition that can be rebuilt. The interior that is currently too disordered to hold what it receives was not always that way, and does not have to stay that way. The rebuilding is real work, and it is not accomplished in a moment. But it is possible. And understanding that it is possible — and that the barrier is structural rather than personal — changes the posture of the person living in the cycle.

Thomas eventually stopped trying to feel the clarity more intensely and started asking a different question. Not how do I hold onto this feeling? But what would need to be true about my interior for this truth to have somewhere permanent to land?

That question is the beginning of formation rather than consumption. It is the beginning of rebuilding rather than recovery. And it is the question that everything which follows is designed to help answer.

Across five chapters, a single picture has been assembled.

God designed the human being for order. He built an interior architecture with a specific sequence — spirit governing, soul following, body expressing. He placed that person in a world of extravagant abundance, blessed them before they had done anything to earn it, and walked with them in the ordinary hours of the day.

Then disorder entered. The sequence is reversed. The ground was cursed. The soul moved to the front, and the spirit fell quiet. Every human being born since has inherited that reversed architecture. He has been experiencing its effects — in the drift, in the fading clarity, in the Sunday-to-Monday distance that feels so personal but is in fact structural.

You have lived every part of this picture.

What you may not yet have is a name for it that is precise enough to produce relief instead of shame. A description specific enough that when you encounter it, you recognize your own experience in it — and realize, perhaps for the first time, that what you have been carrying is not a private failure.

It is a shared human condition with a shared human name.

And a structural solution.

That is what the next chapter gives you.

Part Three: **The Problem Named**

VI

The Gap

"My people are destroyed for lack of knowledge." — Hosea 4:6

On the sixth day, God gave everything.

Before Adam had worked a single hour. Before Eve had made a single decision. Before either of them had done anything to demonstrate faithfulness, consistency, or spiritual readiness, God blessed them. He gave them identity, purpose, provision, dominion, and the unobstructed presence of Himself in the ordinary rhythm of the day. Everything that the H.A.V.E. Effect describes was already in their hands before the first Monday had ever existed.

That is what was lost.

Not in a single dramatic moment of rebellion. In the slow accumulation of everything this book has traced: the architectural reversal, the ground cursed, the governing lights dimmed, the clarity arriving in spaces not yet prepared to hold it. The distance between the Day 6 inheritance and the Monday morning reality — that distance is the gap. It is not a metaphor. It is the most precisely nameable experience in the life of every sincere believer who has ever wondered why Sunday and Monday feel like two different lives.

And that is exactly what this chapter names.

Let's take stock of where we are.

You were designed for a world that no longer exists.

God built the human being for Eden — for an environment where peace was the default condition of life, where alignment was the starting point rather than the destination, where the presence of God was as ordinary as the cool of the day. You were made for a world where spirit led, soul followed, and the body expressed the life flowing through a rightly ordered interior. Not as a spiritual achievement. As the baseline of what human existence was meant to feel like.

That world ended.

Disorder entered through a single reframe — a question that shifted focus from abundance to restriction, from trust to suspicion, from what was given to what was withheld. And in that shift, the interior architecture reversed. The soul moved to the front. The spirit fell quiet. The body began reacting to a world it now experienced as threatening rather than generous. What had been seamless became fractured. What had been effortless became contested.

The fracture passed into every generation that followed. You did not choose it. You inherited it as the condition of being human east of Eden. The disordered sequence — soul leading, spirit struggling to be heard, body reacting from fear rather than expressing peace — is the water you have always swum in. The starting architecture you have always built from, whether you knew it or not.

And then drift entered.

Not through rebellion. Through the quiet mathematics of displacement. Legitimate responsibilities accumulated until the one thing necessary had no room left. Urgency replaced direction, so the transition was gradually invisible. The soul moved further from its anchor across hundreds of ordinary days, none of which felt like a turning point, all of which added up to a significant distance.

Clarity arrived, as it always does — in moments of worship, in seasons of prayer, in passages of Scripture that landed with unmistakable weight. And then it faded. Not because it was false. Because the interior that received it was not structured to hold it. Insight arrived in a disordered soul and could not take permanent root. The mirror showed something true. The moment you looked away, the image was gone.

You have lived every chapter of this.

Not as ancient history. As your own.

The people we have encountered in these pages have not been strangers.

You have met the woman who built her entire adult life around serving others, who gave and gave from a vessel that slowly emptied until the performance of faithfulness outlasted the power of it — who told me she used to feel God in the work and now only felt tired.

You have met the man whose season of loss planted a single quiet question in the center of his identity — not a question about God's power, but about his own place within it — and who kept that question hidden beneath years of continued service until the weight of carrying it in silence became its own kind of collapse.

You have met the man whose anchor slipped so gradually he could not name when the drift began, who was present in every room but reachable in none of them, who still believed God was everywhere but had stopped experiencing Him anywhere.

You have met the man whose life was full of genuinely good things, who put himself consistently in the path of clarity and received it regularly and sincerely, but whose every margin had been filled by something legitimate until the signal God was sending could never break through the noise long enough to take root.

These are not extreme cases. They are not people whose faith failed dramatically or whose character collapsed under obvious pressure. They are ordinary believers living ordinary lives, each of them carrying a gap between the life they experienced in their best moments and the life they inhabited in all the others.

And every one of them, when the gap was named precisely enough that they could recognize their own experience in the description, said some version of the same thing.

"I thought it was just me."

It was not just them. It is not just you.

The gap is not a private failure. It is a shared human condition with a structural cause. And a structural condition is a fundamentally different thing from a character deficiency. You cannot rebuild a character deficiency through greater effort. But a structural condition can be addressed. The architecture that cannot currently hold what it receives can be rebuilt into one that can.

That is the entire premise of what follows.

Here is the question that has been present beneath every chapter.

Why?

Why does genuine faith — sincere, real, not performative — still produce this experience? Why do people who love God, who are not casual or indifferent about their spiritual lives, who show up and engage and genuinely desire to live aligned with what they believe — why do they still find themselves living in two separate registers? Fully present to God in certain conditions and largely absent from that presence in others?

Why does Sunday produce clarity that Monday cannot hold?

The answer most people reach for is self-directed. They are the problem. Their discipline is insufficient. Their faith is weak. Their character has a flaw that makes them less capable of the consistency that other believers seem to manage. They have tried harder and fallen short often enough that the conclusion feels like earned self-knowledge rather than misdiagnosis.

But watch what Jesus said about the seed that fell on rocky ground.

"As for what was sown on rocky ground, this is the one who hears the word and immediately receives it with joy, yet he has no root in himself, but endures for a while, and when tribulation or persecution arises on account of the word, immediately he falls away."

This person received the word. Responded with joy — genuine joy. Endured for a while. The clarity was real. The response was sincere. None of that is in question.

But there was no root.

No structural depth beneath the surface response. And when ordinary pressure arrived — not catastrophic pressure, just the tribulation that is the ordinary texture of life east of Eden — the thing with no root could not hold.

Jesus was not describing a faithless person. He was describing a person whose faith had no structural foundation to grow from. A person in whom clarity arrived, but structure was absent—a person who experienced the Sunday of the parable without the architecture that Monday requires.

The problem is not your faith. The problem is structural.

Hosea named the same reality in a single sentence that has outlasted the civilization for which he wrote.

"My people are destroyed for lack of knowledge."

He was not writing about people who had abandoned God. He was writing about people who maintained the forms of faith — the rituals, the observances, the language of devotion — while living at a significant and growing distance from the reality those forms were meant to express. People who felt the hollowness of going through the motions. Who sensed the gap but could not name it. Those who experienced the distance between their devotion and their daily lives as personal failure rather than a structural condition.

They were destroyed not by rebellion.

By the absence of specific knowledge.

Knowledge of what was actually happening inside them. Knowledge of why the gap kept returning. Knowledge that would have allowed them to address the actual problem rather than working harder at everything around it.

What cannot be named cannot be addressed. What cannot be addressed continues unchanged.

And the people carrying the gap in silence, assuming they are the exception, never discover that the person beside them is carrying the same thing.

Jesus pressed the same diagnosis from a different angle:

"These people honor me with their lips, but their hearts are far from me."

Far. Not absent. Not hostile. Far.

The lips are present. The language is intact. The forms are maintained. But the interior — the heart, the actual governing center of the person — has moved. Gradually. Across many ordinary days. Each one is unremarkable. The distance is visible only when measured against where it started.

This is the pattern no one talks about.

Not because people are hiding it. Because most people have never had language for it precise enough to name it honestly to themselves, let alone to anyone else.

It is worth pausing to name what it actually costs a person to live in the gap for an extended period.

Because the cost is real and rarely discussed honestly.

The most immediate cost is exhaustion. Not physical exhaustion — though that often accompanies it. The particular exhaustion that comes from maintaining a significant gap between internal experience and external expression over a long period of time. The person in the gap is not hypocritical in the sense of deliberate pretense. They are not performing something they know to be false. They genuinely believe what they say they believe. But they are living at a distance from the reality of what they believe, and sustaining that distance — showing up, engaging, participating in the language and community of faith while privately experiencing the hollowness of a life that does not yet match it — is quietly exhausting in a way that is difficult to explain to anyone who has not felt it.

The second cost is loneliness. Not social loneliness — the person in the gap is often deeply embedded in the community. But the particular loneliness of carrying something that feels too shameful to name. Because the dominant narrative of the communities most of these people belong to does not make much room for honest conversation about the gap. The public language of faith emphasizes victory, growth, and transformation. And the person sitting in the service, feeling the distance between that language and their own interior experience, assumes they are alone in the distance. They look at the faces around them and conclude that everyone else has something they are missing. That the gap is their particular failure, not a shared human condition.

That assumption is almost always wrong. But it is very hard to correct in an environment where the gap is never named.

The third cost is gradual disengagement. Not a dramatic departure. The slow withdrawal of the person who has been trying long enough that the trying itself has become its own kind of despair. They continue the forms. They do not leave. But they stop expecting anything to change.

They have moved from hoping for transformation to managing a condition they have concluded is permanent. And in that managed state, they are present in body but increasingly absent in expectation — which means they are present in body but increasingly unavailable to the work God most wants to do in them.

These costs accumulate silently. They are not announced. They do not announce themselves. They settle into the interior over time, layer by layer, until the person carrying them has adjusted so completely to the weight that they have forgotten what it felt like to be without it.

The gap not only keeps people from flourishing. It quietly exhausts the people who carry it.

Here is what every chapter has been building toward.

A single, precise diagnosis.

People do not struggle because they lack faith.

They struggle because their lives are structurally misaligned with their beliefs.

Read that again.

Structurally misaligned.

Not someone who has tried and failed in ways others have not. Not morally compromised. Not insufficiently committed or sincerely lacking

in ways that more devoted believers are not. Structurally misaligned —
meaning the architecture of daily life has not been built to hold what the
spirit receives. Meaning the interior sequence is still operating from the
disorder inherited at the fall rather than from the restored order God
intends. Meaning the gap between Sunday's clarity and Monday's reality
is not primarily a faith problem.

It is a structural one.

The problem is rarely spiritual sincerity. The problem
is structural disorder.

This reframes everything about where effort should go.

A structural problem does not yield to more effort applied to the same
broken structure. A fractured foundation does not become stable under
the weight of more commitment placed on it. Inspiration poured
repeatedly into a vessel not built to retain it, but it does not change the
vessel's capacity.

What is required is not addition. It is reconstruction.

Not more effort applied to the same broken structure. A different kind
of work entirely.

Not the next version of what has already been tried. The first step of
something that has not yet been tried.

And the moment that distinction becomes clear, the entire experience of spiritual inconsistency stops being evidence of personal failure and starts being evidence of something that can actually be addressed.

That shift — from shame to diagnosis, from self-condemnation to structural understanding — is itself a form of freedom. Not the full freedom yet. But the beginning of it.

The distance between what people experience in moments of spiritual clarity and how they live in the ordinary days that follow — that distance has a name.

It is called the Sunday/Monday Gap.

Not a metaphor for the difference between sacred and secular space. Not a critique of how people spend their weekdays. A precise description of a structural reality that lives in the interior of every believer who has ever wondered why faith feels like two different experiences depending on the conditions around them.

Sunday represents the conditions that briefly restore alignment. The environment of worship, Scripture, and community temporarily quiets the disordered soul. The spirit rises to its intended position. The right sequence reasserts itself. God feels near — not because He moved, but because the noise that usually muffles His presence has momentarily softened. Peace returns not as an effort but as a condition. Clarity arrives not as an achievement but as the natural result of a soul briefly operating the way it was designed to.

Monday represents the return of everything else. The ordinary week. The environment that does not naturally support alignment, and never has, east of Eden. The demands reassemble. The pace accelerates. The soul, conditioned by years of operating from the disordered sequence, moves back to the front. The spirit's voice grows faint behind the noise. And the peace that felt so stable twelve hours ago begins to thin.

The gap is the distance between those two experiences.

It is not random. It is not the result of insufficient effort or inadequate faith. It is the structurally inevitable result of a human being whose interior has not yet been rebuilt to hold what Sunday keeps offering. The clarity arrives. The structure to retain it is absent. And so the cycle repeats — Sunday to Monday, clarity to fading, conviction to drift — until either the person accepts the cycle as permanent or discovers that the structure can be rebuilt.

Clarity with God is rarely the problem. Sustaining it is.

The Sunday/Monday Gap is not a new problem. It runs through the entire biblical narrative, dressed in different clothing across different centuries, but always recognizable by its shape.

Israel in the wilderness experienced it with unmistakable clarity. They had witnessed the plagues of Egypt. They had walked through the parted sea on dry ground. They had watched the water return on their pursuers and emerged on the other side singing. And within three days, they were complaining about the water.

Three days. From the miracle to the murmuring.

This is not a story about a faithless people. It is a story about the structural reality of what happens when extraordinary clarity arrives in an interior that has not yet been rebuilt to sustain it. The Red Sea was a Sunday. The wilderness was Monday. And between them, the gap asserted itself with the same quiet inevitability it asserts itself in every human life that has not yet found the anchor that holds.

David wrote Psalm 23 from inside a life that knew both the valley of the shadow of death and the table prepared in the presence of enemies. He was not describing a theory of God's faithfulness. He was describing the lived experience of a man who had found the interior anchor that the wilderness had not yet taught Israel. Not because David was without failure — his record on that front is painfully transparent. But because he had developed something within him that kept returning him to the source whenever the gap asserted itself. He wrote his way back. He prayed his way back. He refused to let the distance become permanent.

The pattern across Scripture is consistent: the gap is the human condition. The return is always possible. And the people who live closest to alignment are not those who never experience the gap, but those who have been rebuilt in their interior so as not to remain in it.

There is a reason this chapter exists before the solutions.

Before anything can be rebuilt, the problem must be accurately named. Not generally — most people already have a general sense that something is wrong. But specifically. With enough precision that the person reading can recognize their own experience in the description and say, with some measure of relief, that this is what has been happening.

That recognition is not a small thing. It is, in fact, one of the most significant movements that can happen in a person's spiritual life. Because the experience of the gap carries enormous shame for most people who carry it, they have concluded, often over many years, that the distance between their Sunday experience and their Monday life is evidence of something fundamentally wrong with them as a person of faith. And that conclusion functions like a weight placed on everything they attempt.

When the gap is named — when a person encounters a description of their experience that is specific and accurate enough that they recognize it without being told — the shame mechanism is interrupted and not eliminated. Not instantly resolved. But interrupted. Because the gap, once named, is no longer a private failure. It is a shared human condition with a specific structural cause. And a structural condition is a very different thing from a character deficiency.

You cannot rebuild a character deficiency. You can only regret it, try harder to overcome it, and brace for the next failure. But a structural condition can be addressed. The structure that currently cannot hold what it receives can be rebuilt into a structure that can. The misaligned interior can be reordered. The architecture that has been running from the fall's disorder can be rebuilt around the restoration God has always been moving toward.

This is what the naming makes possible. Not the rebuilding itself — that is the work of what follows. But the shift in posture makes the rebuilding conceivable. The moment when a person stops trying harder at the same broken approach and begins, for the first time, to look for a different kind of work.

John recorded a promise from Jesus that names exactly what it takes to close the gap.

"If you abide in my word, you are truly my disciples, and you will know the truth, and the truth will set you free."

The condition is abiding and not hearing. Not receiving with joy and not enduring for a while.

Abiding — remaining, staying, building a life structured in such a way that what has been received does not drift to the periphery when ordinary conditions return.

To abide carries the sense of taking up permanent residence, not visiting or passing through, and of making a home in something and structuring your life in such a way that the truth you have received is not a guest that comes and goes but a resident that shapes everything about how the house is ordered.

This is not a discipline maintained through effort. It is the natural expression of an interior that has been rebuilt to hold what it receives. It is what happens when the structure finally matches the clarity. When the foundation is solid enough that Monday's pressure does not dislodge what Sunday produced. When the person who sat in the service and received the clarity carries it, it is not because they are gripping it tightly, but because the structure of their interior has been rebuilt so that carrying it becomes the path of least resistance.

Abiding is not a spiritual achievement reserved for advanced believers. It is a description of what a rightly ordered interior does naturally. The soul that has been rebuilt around God's governance does not have to work to remain in His word any more than a tree planted by water has to work to remain watered. The structure provides what the effort never could.

The truth sets free. But only the truth that remains.

The Sunday/Monday Gap is the experience of receiving truth that does not yet remain. Of touching freedom repeatedly without yet inhabiting it. Of living close enough to alignment to know what it feels like, but not yet in the structural condition to sustain it.

That condition can change.

That is the entire premise of what follows.

If you have recognized yourself in these pages, something significant has happened.

You now have language for an experience you have been carrying without it. And that matters more than it might seem in this moment, because language changes your relationship to an experience. The gap that has no name feels like a permanent personal failing. The gap that has a name feels like a condition that can be understood — and therefore addressed.

You are not broken.

You are not spiritually deficient. You are not the exception among believers who somehow cannot manage what everyone else handles without difficulty. You are a human being with an inherited interior disorder, living in a world structurally hostile to alignment, experiencing the precise and predictable gap that results when those two realities collide with genuine faith.

Every sincere believer who has ever sat in a service and felt the clarity arrive — and then watched it fade before the week was out — has been living this gap. The high-capacity leader who seems to have it together. The longtime church member whose consistency looks effortless from the outside. The new believer whose faith still has the brightness of something recently discovered. The gap is present across all of them, in varying forms and depths.

You are not alone in it.

You are not uniquely weak because of it.

And it does not have to be permanent.

When faith and life move together, stability follows.

The gap has a name. And now that it has been named, the rebuilding can begin.

That is where the next chapter takes you.

No more diagnoses. The first movement of reconstruction.

Part Four: **The Turn**

VII

Rebuilding Order

"Seek first the kingdom of God and his righteousness, and all these things will be added to you." — Matthew 6:33

God does not build differently than He ever has.

When He made the world, He followed a sequence. Light before life. Foundation before filling. Structure before abundance. He did not rush. He did not skip steps. He did not pour life into spaces that had not yet been prepared to receive it. Every layer was laid before the next one was added, and nothing was placed on a foundation that had not first been secured.

When He rebuilds the human interior, He follows the same sequence.

This matters more than most people realize when they begin the work of restoration. Because the instinct — formed by years of trying to fix the symptoms rather than the structure — is to reach for the visible, change the behavior. Add the discipline. Recommit to the practices. Start at the top and work down.

But God always starts at the bottom. He always addresses the foundation first. He is not interested in a life that looks ordered from the outside while the interior remains disordered beneath the surface. He is interested in a rebuilt foundation — the kind that holds not because it is being held together by effort, but because the structure beneath it has been genuinely restored.

The chapters that follow this one describe what begins to emerge when that foundation is being rebuilt. Four things. Each one is a natural expression of restored interior order. Each one is evidence that the gap is closing.

But before those things can emerge, the rebuilding itself has to begin. And the rebuilding always begins in the same place it always has — not with what you do, but with what God initiates.

You have carried this longer than you should have had to carry it alone.

The gap between who you are on Sunday and who you are on Monday. The conviction that fades before the week is done. The clarity that arrives with such force and then retreats so quietly, you are never sure exactly when it leaves—the private exhaustion of trying to hold together an interior life that keeps wanting to fall apart.

You carried it quietly, mostly. You managed to convey a sense of consistency even when the interior felt anything but. You recommitted more times than you can count, with genuine intention each time, and felt the particular discouragement of watching the cycle return despite the sincerity of the effort.

And somewhere along the way, without deciding to, you began to accept it as the permanent condition of your life.

That acceptance was not weakness. It was a reasonable conclusion of a person who had tried every available solution and found none sufficient. When the tools you have do not fix the problem, the human response is to stop believing the problem can be fixed eventually.

But the tools weren't wrong; you just used them poorly.

They were wrong because they were addressing the wrong problem.

You were trying to manage symptoms of a structural disorder. And structural disorders do not respond to symptom management. They require something different. Something that goes beneath the surface of behavior and habit, and of renewed commitment, and reaches the architecture itself.

That is what this chapter is about.

Not a new set of practices. Not a better version of what you have already tried.

The beginning of a different kind of work entirely.

Before we talk about what rebuilding order requires of you, it is essential to establish what it requires of God.

Because the order of that sequence matters more than most people realize.

The instinct, when confronted with a structural problem, is to ask what needs to be done immediately. What steps. What changes. What disciplines need to be added, replaced, or intensified? The performance orientation that the fall introduced runs deep — the soul's default assumption is that restoration is something you produce through sufficient effort.

But Scripture consistently reverses that sequence.

God does not wait for human beings to reconstruct their own interior order before He moves toward them. He moves first. He has always moved first. Before Adam and Eve had taken a single step toward repair, God was already walking in the garden, already asking the question that would begin the process of drawing them back, already preparing the covering that would restore what shame had stripped.

The first sacrifice in Scripture was not human effort reaching toward God.

It was God reaching toward human need.

That pattern runs unbroken through every act of restoration in the biblical narrative. It is not the person who gets themselves sufficiently together and then receives God's help. It is God who initiates, who creates the conditions for restoration, who does the work that human effort cannot do — and then invites the person into participation with what He has already begun.

Moses did not work his way back to God from the backside of the desert. God came to Moses. The bush was burning before Moses turned to look.

The prodigal son's father did not wait for his son to complete the journey and demonstrate adequate repentance before responding. He saw him when he was still a great way off and ran.

Peter, standing on the shore after the resurrection, drying out from the swim he had made when he recognized the Lord, Jesus did not wait for Peter to sort out his shame from the denial before He spoke to him. He had already prepared the fire and already prepared the meal. The restoration was being cooked before Peter arrived.

This is not a pattern of exceptions. It is the consistent logic of how God moves toward the people He is rebuilding. He arrives first. He prepares the conditions. He initiates the work. And then He invites the person into the participation that will make the rebuilding real in their lived experience.

Peace returns when life is reordered around God.

This matters because it changes the posture with which rebuilding begins.

You do not begin from zero. You do not begin alone. You do not begin by constructing something new from raw materials; you have to gather them through sufficient discipline and consistency.

You begin by receiving what God has already initiated.

The invitation to rebuild is not a challenge to your willpower. It is a response to work that is already underway. God is not waiting at the destination for you to arrive through your own effort. He is present at the beginning, at the place where the disorder is most visible, most raw, most honest — and He starts there.

Where you are is always where restoration begins.

Not where you should be. Not where you intend to be.

Where you are.

And yet.

Receiving is not passive.

There is a waiting that looks like faith but is actually avoidance — an indefinite postponement of the participation that restoration requires. God initiates. He always initiates. But rebuilding is not something He does entirely to a motionless person. It is something He does with a person who has turned toward the work.

The distinction matters. The person who understands that God moves first can receive that truth as permission for continued inaction — if God will do the work, then the work does not require anything from me. That is a misreading. God's prior movement is not a replacement for human participation. It is the ground on which participation becomes possible.

A tree does not grow itself. But it does grow. The conditions that make growth possible — soil, water, light — are not produced by the tree's effort. But the tree still has to be planted in them. It still has to be in the right soil, receiving the right light, and positioned to draw from the water. The conditions are provided. The positioning is the tree's participation.

Rebuilding order works the same way. God provides the conditions. The person participates by positioning themselves in them — by turning toward the work, by making available the interior space where the rebuilding can happen, by ceasing the management strategies that have been compensating for the structural disorder and allowing the disorder itself to be addressed.

That positioning is not passive. It is the most active thing a person can do. Because it requires abandoning the familiar management strategies that feel like effort but are actually forms of avoidance. It requires the willingness to be in the discomfort of the transition between what was and what is being rebuilt. It requires showing up, repeatedly, to the ordinary work of reorientation when every formed habit of the interior pulls toward what is already established.

The Psalter is full of people who had been through everything this book has described — the disorder, the drift, the fading clarity, the exhaustion of living in the gap — and who had arrived at a moment of specific, costly reorientation. Not a recommitment to the same things. A turning. A deliberate repositioning of what stood at the center.

Moses, near the end of his life, prayed something that has outlasted everything else he accomplished:

"Teach us to number our days, that we may gain a heart of wisdom."

Teach us to number our days.

It is a request to see time accurately. Not to manage it more efficiently. Not to optimize it toward better outcomes. To see it for what it is — finite, unrepeatable, moving in one direction only — so that the choices made within it are shaped by that reality rather than by the illusion of unlimited time that allows indefinite postponement of what actually matters.

A person who numbers their days does not defer alignment indefinitely. They understand that the day they are currently living is the only version of that day that will ever exist. The clarity available right now, in this moment, is not guaranteed to return in the same form at a more convenient time. The reconstruction of the inner life is not a project that can wait until circumstances are more favorable.

There is no more favorable time.

There is only now, and what is done with it.

Transformation does not begin with trying harder. It begins with rebuilding order.

Paul wrote to the Corinthians that everything in the life of faith should be done "decently and in order." That instruction is often applied to church services. But its principle extends into every dimension of the aligned life.

Order is not a restriction. It is the condition under which things function as they were designed to function. A river without banks is not freer — it is a flood. A life without the ordering of priorities around what matters most is not more expansive — it is scattered.

Order is what makes abundance possible.

And the rebuilding order begins with a single, specific reorientation that Jesus described more clearly than anyone else has before or since.

"Seek first the kingdom of God and his righteousness, and all these things will be added to you."

First.

Not eventually. Not when the other priorities have been addressed. Not as one important thing among several important things. First, it is the governing center around which everything else is arranged, as the thing that determines the sequence of everything that follows it.

The word translated "seek" carries the sense of active pursuit. Deliberate orientation. The turning of the whole person — attention, desire, time, energy — toward a specific object. Jesus was not describing a passive awareness of God's kingdom. He was describing a life structurally arranged around it.

This is the challenge of rebuilding.

Not the addition of spiritual practices to an already full life. The reordering of what already exists around a new center. Not squeezing God into the margins of a structure that was built around everything else. Rebuilding the structure itself so that what is first is actually first — not just in stated priority, but in the daily, practical arrangement of attention and time and energy.

That reordering is costly. It requires things that have been settled in certain positions for a long time to move. Habits that have accumulated around the wrong center. Patterns of attention that have formed around urgency rather than direction. An interior life that has spent years governed by the soul's self-protective instincts rather than the spirit's God-directed clarity.

None of that moves without intention.

But intention, when it is aligned with what God has already initiated, is not the same as striving. It is cooperation. It is the person who turns to face the direction God is already moving in and begins to walk.

Alignment changes what effort cannot.

It is worth being concrete about what reordering around "first" actually requires in a lived life.

Because the instruction is easy to affirm in the abstract and remarkably difficult to act on in the specific, most believers already believe that God should be first. The gap is not between the belief and the correct answer. The gap is between the stated priority and the actual structure of the day.

When Jesus said to seek first the kingdom, He was describing a life in which the governing question of each day is not what needs to get done, but what God is doing and how this day participates in it. That is a genuinely different orientation than the one most people operate from. Most people begin the day from the position of their own agenda — the demands, the schedule, the accumulated obligations — and try to fit God into the margins. Not because they intend to marginalize God. Because the structure of the day was built around the demands before it was built around Him, and restructuring it requires a deliberate act of reordering that most people never quite get around to.

What has to move, concretely, is the governing question.

Not the schedule, necessarily — though the schedule often follows. Not the activities, though those often shift too. The question that organizes the interior as the day begins. The frame through which the ordinary hours are interpreted. The lens that determines which inputs are treated as essential and which as noise.

A day organized around the question "What needs to get done?" produces a productive person, but one who is often empty. Effective at the level of output but chronically undernourished at the level of the interior. Always moving, rarely settled. Accomplishing a great deal while experiencing a persistent sense that none of it is adding up to anything that actually matters.

A day organized around the question "What is God doing, and how am I participating in it?" produces a person who brings a different quality to the same activities. Not less productive. Often more so, because the anxiety that drives much of the frantic productivity is no longer in the governing position. But differently oriented. Moving from a center rather than being driven by a current. Present in a way that the agenda-governed person rarely is, because the governing frame is larger than the immediate demands and therefore not consumed by them.

This reorientation does not happen in a single morning. It is the work of months of deliberate return to the governing question, gradually displacing the performance orientation that has been governing the interior for years. But each return matters. Each day that begins with the right question is a day in which the structure of the interior is reinforced rather than eroded. And over time, the cumulative effect of those days is a life that has actually been reordered around what was always meant to be first.

Proverbs 4 contains an instruction so practical that it is easy to underestimate:

"Let your eyes look directly forward, and your gaze be straight before you. Ponder the path of your feet; then all your ways will be sure. Do not swerve to the right or to the left; turn your foot away from evil."

Ponder the path of your feet.

Not the path of your aspirations. Not the path of your intentions. The actual path your feet are currently walking. The real direction your life is moving, assessed honestly against the direction you believe it should be going.

This is one of the most underutilized practices in the life of faith — not because it is difficult to understand, but because honest self-assessment is uncomfortable. It requires looking at the distance between what is stated and what is actual. Between the values declared and the choices made, between the life described on Sunday and the life lived on Monday.

Most people avoid that assessment because they fear what they will find. But the proverb promises something remarkable to the person who does it: all your ways will be sure. Not all your circumstances will be comfortable. Not all your outcomes will be favorable. Your ways will be sure — your direction will be clear, your footing will be solid, and the path you are walking will be the path you actually intend to walk.

That sureness is what the aligned life feels like from the inside. Not the absence of difficulty. The presence of a direction that holds even when circumstances change.

The person who has been living in the gap tends to approach self-assessment with either avoidance or condemnation. They either don't look or, if they do, they punish themselves for what they see. Both responses keep the path unclear. Avoidance because the honest assessment never happens. Condemnation because it replaces the useful diagnostic information with shame that paralyzes rather than redirects.

The proverb is offering a third option. Look honestly. Not to confirm a verdict about yourself, but to get an accurate reading of your actual direction. Then adjust. Not with self-punishment, not with dramatic recommitment, but with the quiet, practical reorientation of a person who checked their compass, found they had drifted a few degrees off course, and corrected.

That correction, repeated regularly, is one of the most powerful structural practices available to the person who is rebuilding order. Not because it feels significant in any individual instance. But because the cumulative effect of small course corrections, made faithfully over time, produces a life that is actually walking in the direction it intends to walk.

There is a pattern in how Scripture describes the process of restoration that is worth naming explicitly, because it runs counter to the intuitions most people bring to the work.

The pattern is this: God restores from the inside out.

The human instinct is to work from the outside in. Change the behavior first, and hope the interior follows. Get the disciplines in place, and trust that the interior will gradually align with them. Shape the external life into a form that appears aligned, and believe that the appearance will eventually become reality.

This approach produces real results at the surface level. The person who implements external disciplines is genuinely better off than the person who does nothing. The practices carry real value. But they do not reach the disorder. They improve the performance without rebuilding the architecture. And because the architecture remains disordered, the disciplines require constant maintenance — they must be held in place by effort, because the interior structure beneath them is still pulling in a different direction.

God works differently.

Ezekiel recorded a promise from God that describes the direction of His restoration work with unusual precision:

"I will give you a new heart and put a new spirit in you; I will remove from you your heart of stone and give you a heart of flesh. And I will put my Spirit in you and move you to follow my decrees and be careful to keep my laws."

The sequence is internal first. New heart. New spirit. The Spirit is placed within. And then — as a consequence of that interior work, not as a precondition for it — the person begins to follow. Obedience is the result of an interior change, not its cause.

This does not mean external practices are irrelevant. They are not. But it means their proper function is as a response to interior work, not a substitute for it. The person who prays, reads Scripture, and gathers with community because those practices are the natural expression of an interior that has been reordered — that person is building on a foundation. The person who does those same things, hoping that doing them will eventually produce the interior they have not yet received, is still working outside in and will continue to find the work more effortful than it was designed to be.

The question rebuilding order asks is not "What should I be doing?" It is "What is God doing in me, and how do I position myself to receive it fully?"

That is a different question. It produces different work. And it leads to a different outcome.

Order, once it begins to return, feels less like an achievement and more like coming home.

Most books about spiritual reconstruction describe the work. Fewer describe what the work produces in the interior as it begins to take hold.

That interior experience is worth naming, because it is often subtler than people expect. The person who has been living in the gap for years tends to anticipate that restoration will arrive with the same emotional intensity as the moments of clarity that have been arriving and fading for so long. They are waiting for an experience that feels definitively different. A moment of breakthrough. A dramatic shift in the interior landscape that announces, unmistakably, that something has changed.

The experience of order beginning to return is usually quieter than that.

It begins as a kind of steadiness that was not there before. Not excitement. Not the heightened awareness of a spiritual high. Just steadiness. The Monday morning that used to arrive with the weight of a returning distance between the person and everything the Sunday before had offered — that Monday morning is slightly different—not transformed. Slightly different. The weight is a little lighter. The distance feels a little less automatic. The capacity to carry the ordinary demands of the day without losing the interior sense of being held by something larger than the demands — that capacity has increased, almost imperceptibly, since the last time the person checked.

Over weeks and months, that steadiness deepens. The person begins to notice that the clarity-fade cycle, while not completely gone, is operating on a different timeline. The clarity from Sunday is still present on Wednesday, in a way it wasn't before. The conviction that formed in prayer is still shaping decisions on Friday in a way it would have blurred by Tuesday in an earlier season. The gap is narrowing. Not because the person has worked harder. Because the structure has been quietly changing underneath the ordinary days.

There is also a change in the quality of the person's presence — to themselves, to God, to the people around them. The scattered, surface-level engagement that characterizes the person living in the gap begins to give way to something more available. More there. The people closest to them notice it before the person themselves does. A quality of groundedness that was not present before. The person's own interior begins to feel less like a contested space and more like a governed one — less like a room where too many things are competing for the role of governing, and more like a room put in order.

Peace is often the first word people reach for when describing what the early stages of restored alignment feel like. Not the absence of pressure — the pressure is still there. But a quality of stability beneath the pressure that makes it possible to carry the pressure without being governed by it. The ordinary demands of the week have not changed. But the interior carrying them has. And the difference between a soul that is carrying the week from a place of order and a soul that is being carried by the week from a place of disorder — that difference is precisely what the word peace describes.

These are not guarantees of a linear progression without setbacks. Rebuilding order is not a smooth upward trajectory. It involves seasons of clarity and seasons of difficulty, periods of significant progress and periods where the drift seems to reassert itself. But the person who has begun the actual structural work experiences those difficult seasons differently than they did before. The drift, when it returns, is recognized more quickly. The distance, when it opens, is named more accurately. The return to center, when it is needed, is less disorienting — because the center has become more established, and the path back to it more familiar.

Here is what makes the work of rebuilding fundamentally different from every previous attempt at spiritual consistency.

You are not doing it alone.

You are not doing it with tools that were insufficient before and will remain so. You are not attempting to reconstruct from the outside in — behavior first, interior second — which has never produced lasting change for anyone, because that is not how the human being was designed to be rebuilt.

You are participating in a work that God initiates, sustains, and completes.

Paul described the nature of that work to the Philippians with a confidence that was not naive optimism — it was the confidence of a man who had watched God finish what He started in human lives across decades of ministry:

"He who began a good work in you will carry it on to completion until the day of Christ Jesus."

He who began.

Not he who will begin once you have sufficiently prepared yourself. Not he who will begin, once you have demonstrated adequate commitment. He who began — past tense, already in motion, already underway in the interior of the person reading this sentence.

The work of rebuilding your order has already started.

It started the moment you began to feel the weight of the gap. It started in the seasons of clarity that arrived even though the structure to hold them was not yet in place. It started in the longing for a life that holds together, a longing that has persisted through every cycle of drift and recommitment. That longing is not self-generated. It is the evidence of a God who has been working in the interior long before the person had language for what He was doing.

Peace returns when life is reordered around God.

What changes now is not the presence of God's work. What changes is your cooperation with it.

The person who understands that the gap is structural — not personal, not permanent — approaches the work of rebuilding differently than the person who believes they are simply trying again at the same thing that failed before. They bring honesty instead of performance. Participation instead of striving. A willingness to be rebuilt rather than a determination to rebuild themselves.

That posture is everything.

Because it is precisely the posture in which God does His deepest work. Not in the person who has it together. In the person who has stopped pretending they do, and has turned — with whatever they have, from wherever they are — toward the One who rebuilds what disorder broke.

Rebuilding order is not a single event. It is a direction.

It begins with the honest assessment that the current structure is not working — that Sunday's clarity and Monday's reality have been two different experiences for long enough that the gap can no longer be called temporary. It continues with the deliberate reorientation of what sits at the center of daily life. And it unfolds, gradually, as the interior begins to experience what it was always designed for: spirit leading, soul following, and the peace that is the natural result of that sequence reasserting itself.

That unfolding is not instant. Structures rebuilt from the inside out do not transform overnight. But they do transform. And the transformation, once it begins, is not the fragile, temporary clarity that has faded so many times before.

It is something more durable.

Something that holds.

The chapters that follow describe what begins to emerge in a life that has reoriented around God's order. Not as a set of outcomes to be achieved. This is a description of what becomes naturally possible when the structure that was always meant to hold them is finally in place.

Four things, specifically.

Each one is the result of restored alignment. Each piece of evidence shows that the gap is closing. Each one — and this is what the next chapter begins to reveal — already given to you on the sixth day, before your first Monday had ever existed.

The first one to return is always the same.

It is the one that makes everything else possible.

Part Five: **What Was Always Yours**

VIII

Hope: The First Evidence of Alignment

"May the God of hope fill you with all joy and peace as you trust in him, so that you may overflow with hope by the power of the Holy Spirit." —
Romans 15:13

On the sixth day, before Adam had worked a single hour, God blessed him.

Not instructed. Not warned. Not evaluated. Blessed. The first thing God did toward the human being He had just created was to pour out blessing over a life that had not yet done anything to earn it. Identity. Purpose. Provision. Dominion. Relationship. Everything that would be needed was given before the need was ever felt.

That is the origin of hope.

Not the feeling of optimism that arrives when circumstances are favorable. Not the decision to believe things will work out. Something structurally older than either of those — the cord that was attached before the first Monday existed, running from the human soul to the fixed point of God's own character and provision. Adam did not generate hope. He was given it. He woke up on Day 6 already connected to a source that did not depend on what the week would bring.

The H.A.V.E. Effect begins here. Not because hope is the most dramatic of the four — it isn't. But because it is the first thing that returns when the interior begins to reorder. And it is the only thing that makes the other three receivable.

A soul that has not had its hope restored cannot receive abundance. It filters every provision through the lens of scarcity before it can be received. It cannot sustain virtue, because character that holds under pressure requires a governing center that is not organized around fear. And it cannot access empowerment — because the forward motion that empowerment produces requires a soul that is not bracing against what comes next.

Hope opens everything. It is always what God restores first.

And when alignment begins to return, it is always the first thing the interior recognizes.

Restoration does not announce itself.

It does not arrive with a dramatic moment that leaves no room for doubt. It does not produce a version of you that is suddenly free of struggle, immune to pressure, visibly transformed in every interaction. The rebuilt interior does not come with a certificate of completion or a clear before-and-after line you can point to and say, "That is when everything changed."

What it produces is subtler than that. And more durable.

The first thing to return is not peace, not clarity, not the sustained consistency that has felt so out of reach for so long. The first thing to return is something quieter than all of those. Something that arrives before the person even has language for what they are experiencing.

The first thing to return is hope.

Not optimism. Not the performance of positive thinking. Not the decision to believe things will work out. Something structurally different from all of those. Something that arrives in the interior the way light enters a room — not all at once, not with announcement, but gradually, until the dark room is no longer dark, and the person standing in it realizes they can see again.

Hope is always the first movement of God toward a disordered soul.

Before He restores structure, before He rebuilds capacity, before He brings the clarity that Sunday keeps offering and Monday keeps losing, He begins by awakening hope. Not as encouragement. As reconstruction. Hope enters the places where collapse has become normal and begins quietly, gently, and consistently repairing what disorder has broken. It is not a feeling. It is the first stone God places in the rebuilding of the interior life.

This distinction matters more than it might seem. A feeling can be generated. It can be performed, sustained by willpower for as long as willpower holds, and then lost when the pressure exceeds what willpower can contain. What God produces in the restored interior is not a feeling that must be maintained. It is a structural reorientation — a shift in the governing posture of the soul that holds not because the person is working to hold it, but because the thing it is anchored to does not move.

The Hebrew word for hope is *tikvah*. It means cord, or line. Something attached. A rope that runs from the present moment to a fixed point and remains taut because the fixed point is real.

When the writer of Proverbs says there is a future, and your hope will not be cut off, the word is *tikvah* — your cord is not severed. You are still attached to what you are moving toward. The image is not primarily emotional. It is structural. The cord either holds or it does not. The fixed point either exists or it does not. The question is not whether the person feels hopeful. The question is whether the cord is attached to something real.

This is precisely what the disordered soul loses access to. Not the future itself. But there is a sense of being attached to it by something reliable. The disordered soul experiences time as a series of unconnected presents, each one to be managed as it arrives, without the steady awareness of a cord running toward a fixed point that holds even when the present moment is chaotic. Every day is managed in isolation. Every difficulty is faced as though there is no trajectory, no direction, no One at the other end of the line pulling the present toward something better than what it currently is.

The exhaustion this produces is not primarily physical, though it expresses itself physically. It is the exhaustion of a soul perpetually managing its own weight without the tautness of the cord to carry any of it. The soul was not designed to bear its own weight alone. It was designed to be held — attached to a fixed point that gives the present moment direction and the difficult season a context that is larger than the difficulty itself.

When alignment begins to return, the cord is felt again. Not dramatically. Not as a sudden arrival of certainty about what the future holds. But as a quiet reestablishment of the interior sense that the present moment is not all there is, and that what it is moving toward is being held by Someone whose grip does not depend on how the present moment happens to feel.

Paul called God the God of hope — not merely a God who provides hope as one resource among others, but a God whose very nature is the source of it. When the soul reorients around Him, access to the God of hope is restored in a way it could not be when the interior was disordered. The channel was always there. The structural disorder was blocking it. When the block begins to clear, hope does not have to be manufactured or decided into existence. It simply begins to flow, as water does when the obstruction is removed.

This is important because so much of what believers attempt to do with hope is generate it. The motivational language of faith culture is often aimed at producing a sense of hope through the intensity of its declarations or the elevation of emotion. And there is nothing wrong with declarations or with elevated moments of encounter. But what the restored soul discovers is that it does not have to generate what has begun to flow naturally. The hope is not the product of effort. It is evidence of alignment. It is the cord being felt again because the interior has been reordered around the One to whom it is attached.

Hope is not wishful thinking. It is the soul's first evidence that alignment has begun.

The return of hope is experienced as a gradual loosening rather than a sudden arrival. The held breath is released. The braced interior softens by degrees. The quiet internal conclusion that collapse is not the only possible outcome begins, slowly, to give way. The psalmist described this from the inside: "Why are you cast down, O my soul, and why are you in turmoil within me? Hope in God; for I shall again praise him." He was not commanding a feeling. He was redirecting the governing center of his attention from his circumstances to the character of God.

That redirection is what becomes possible when the interior begins to reorder. The soul in disorder interprets everything through the lens of its own fear. God's silence reads as disinterest. His timing reads as neglect. His process reads as abandonment. The spirit knows better, but the soul's disordered interpretive framework overrides what the spirit carries. When hope returns, that misreading begins to correct itself. God becomes visible again as He actually is — steadier than circumstances, kinder than outcomes, nearer than confusion.

And when God is seen accurately, everything else in the life of faith becomes more navigable.

Every believer knows what it is to lose hope, even if they never say the word aloud.

Losing hope is not always dramatic. It rarely announces itself as a crisis of faith or a moment of conscious surrender. It shows up as a quiet resignation — the internal conclusion, formed slowly over years, that certain cycles cannot break, certain patterns cannot shift, certain wounds will always remain tender, certain areas of life will always stay fragile. The spirit knows God is able. But the soul becomes quietly, persistently convinced that His ability is reserved for others. That the testimonies in the room are for a category of person the soul does not quite qualify as, the gap between what is believed on Sunday and what is experienced on Monday is simply the permanent condition of a person like this, living a life like this, carrying a history like this.

The body responds to this conclusion by tightening. By guarding. By bracing at the slightest pressure, not because the person is faithless but because the soul has learned, through years of experience, that bracing is the most reliable preparation for what tends to happen next.

This is not rebellion. It is collapsing. A collapse formed slowly over years of disappointment, unmet expectation, and the constant low-grade strain of trying to live a life the soul was never equipped to sustain without divine order supporting it from within.

Hope enters precisely at this point — not when the believer is strong, steady, disciplined, or confident, but when the soul has reached the limits of its own capacity. It does not require readiness. It creates readiness. It does not wait for the soul to stabilize. It stabilizes the soul. It opens the interior windows of the heart and lets breath return to places that had learned to inhale fear more easily than they had inhale promise. The soul begins to loosen from positions it has held for so long that it forgot they were positions — began treating them as simply the shape of things, the permanent architecture of its interior life.

When hope begins its work, it rarely announces itself. It begins as the slightest shift — the heaviness loosening a fraction, the thoughts slowing enough to catch one clear word from God, the heart remembering that collapse is not its only familiar pattern. This is why hope is so consistently underestimated. Believers expect transformation to begin with strength, boldness, clarity, or spiritual intensity. But God rebuilds the human soul the same way He rebuilt creation: with light. A single interruption in the chaos reveals that chaos is not permanent. A single moment in which the soul, instead of bracing, breathes.

Hope is always the first movement of God toward a disordered soul.

Hope also confronts the lies the soul adopted while living east of Eden. Disorder trains a believer to expect disappointment, to anticipate collapse, to assume that pressure will always overpower peace. When alignment begins to restore hope, it is not simply encouraging the believer—it is challenging the internal predictions that have been shaping their reactions for years without their conscious awareness. The soul begins to learn, slowly and with some resistance, that its instincts are not infallible and that its fear is not prophetic. Hope interrupts the sequence the believer has repeated for years — the drop in the stomach, the tightening of the chest, the racing of the mind, the shrinking of capacity, the quiet conclusion that this cannot be held. When hope enters, the sequence does not complete itself in the same way. Something slows. Something breathes. Something yields where yielding had not been possible before.

Hope works gently, but it works deeply. It reaches into the places where disappointment sedimented in layers and formed entire belief systems. It touches grief that was never resolved, prayers that felt unanswered, efforts that seemed wasted, seasons of obedience that did not yield visible fruit, and hidden stories of being overlooked, misunderstood, or mishandled. The soul may not be able to articulate these memories. But it carries the emotional weight of them in every new situation that remotely resembles the old ones. Hope does not erase these experiences. It reframes them — so that the soul can release them from the throne where they once sat as judges over the believer's future. Hope dethrones the past. It silences the old verdicts. It tells the soul that it is allowed to expect God again — not as a theological statement, not as an affirmation to be repeated until it feels true, but as a lived, embodied reality that begins to shape the posture of every subsequent day.

Job's story is the most sustained biblical record of what hope looks like when it is tested by the complete removal of everything that normally sustains it.

He had wealth, family, health, reputation, and the explicit acknowledgment of God that he was blameless and upright. By every external measure, Job's life was evidence that faithfulness and divine favor could coexist in visible, tangible ways. And then, across a single sequence of devastating days, all of it was stripped away. His livestock is gone. His servants are gone. His children are gone. Then his health — his body covered with painful sores from the sole of his foot to the crown of his head, so that the physical experience of being alive became a constant source of suffering. Then, the encouragement of his wife, who could not bear to watch what was happening, told him to curse God and die. Then the counsel of his friends, who initially came with sympathy and stayed to deliver a verdict: your suffering is the consequence of hidden sin, because God does not allow this to happen to people who have not done anything to deserve it.

Job was left with nothing external to support his hope. And the question that suffering always produces in a soul that genuinely loved God before the suffering arrived surfaced with full force: Where is He now?

Job did not answer that question quickly. The book that bears his name is not a story of rapid resolution. It is a long, honest, often anguished wrestling with the gap between what Job knew about God and what his circumstances were telling him. He expressed the full range of what a person feels when hope is at its most tested — anger that his righteousness had not protected him, confusion about what the rules of divine engagement actually were, longing for direct audience with God, the suspicion that the audience might not go the way he hoped, the exhaustion of not knowing when any of this would end, and moments of such deep despair that he wished he had never been born.

The friends offered explanations. They were not malicious people. They were operating from the most coherent theological framework available to them: suffering is a consequence, obedience is protection, if you are suffering this badly, there must be something you are not seeing or not admitting. Their explanations were wrong, not because they were foolish, but because they were too small. They were trying to fit what was happening to Job into a framework that could not contain it. And in doing so, they added to his suffering by insisting that the framework was correct and Job's experience must conform to it.

Job refused, not out of arrogance, but out of integrity. He knew his own life. He knew he had not done what they were accusing him of. And he would not confess what was not true to make the theology tidy. This refusal to pretend — this insistence on the honest account of his experience, even when the honest account made everyone uncomfortable — is itself a form of hope. It is the refusal to accept the framework that says God cannot be trusted unless He behaves in ways that are predictable and explainable. Job was holding onto something that could not yet be named — holding onto the Person, even when the Person's behavior made no sense.

And then, from the depths of a man who had lost everything and been abandoned by every human explanation of his suffering, came this:

"For I know that my Redeemer lives, and at the last he will stand upon the earth. And after my skin has been thus destroyed, yet in my flesh I shall see God."

This was not optimism. Job had nothing external to be optimistic about. It was *tikvah* — the cord still taut, still running toward a fixed point, even though everything visible had been stripped away. The fixed point was not Job's circumstances. It was not his health or his wealth or his reputation or his theological coherence. It was the living Redeemer. And that point did not move when everything else did.

*Hope that has been tested is not weaker than hope that
has not. It is more deeply anchored.*

The resolution of Job's story is not the primary point. The primary point is what happened in the interior during the long middle section — the sustained, honest, sometimes furious engagement with a God who seemed silent, from a soul that refused to let the silence become the final word. Job argued. He questioned. He expressed things that made his friends deeply uncomfortable and that have made readers uncomfortable for thousands of years. But he did not stop addressing God. He did not turn his back. He stayed in the conversation even when the conversation felt entirely one-sided, even when the silence felt like evidence that no one was listening, even when the most theologically sophisticated people in his life were insisting that his suffering proved God was against him.

That staying is the shape of hope under pressure. Not the performance of cheerful confidence. The refusal to let the distance become permanent. The soul continues to turn toward the One it knows is there, even when the evidence of His presence is not yet visible in the circumstances.

When God finally spoke from the whirlwind, He did not answer Job's questions. He revealed His own character. He took Job on a tour of the created order — the foundations of the earth, the ordinances of the heavens, the behavior of creatures that Job had never seen and could not begin to comprehend — not to humiliate him but to expand his frame. To show him that the God he was addressing governed a reality so vast and so ordered and so full of intentional design that the suffering of one man, as real and as devastating as it was, existed within a context that Job had never been able to see from where he stood.

Job's response was not the resolution of his questions. It was something better.

"I had heard of you by the hearing of the ear, but now my eye sees you."

The knowledge that had been secondhand became firsthand. The hope that had been inherited became experiential. The God who had been a theological proposition became a present reality — not because the circumstances improved, but because the encounter itself was the thing Job had been reaching for through all the wrestling and all the waiting.

And out of that encounter, the cord was not just held. It was deepened. Refined. Made into something that the next season of difficulty, whatever form it took, could not cut.

The restoration that followed — the wealth returned in double, the new family, the extended years — was not the point. The point was the interior that received the restoration. The Job who received it was not the same as the Job who had it before. Before, abundance had been the context in which his faith operated. After, faith was the context in which abundance arrived. That sequence is the difference between a life built on what God gives and a life built on who God is. And hope — the cord held through the long dark middle when there was nothing external to hold it with — was what produced the interior capable of receiving what came next.

The Psalms are the most honest record available of what hope looks like in the interior of a person who genuinely loves God but is living in a world that does not cooperate with that love.

Psalm 42 opens with thirst. Not metaphorical thirst — the visceral, embodied longing of a creature that needs what it does not currently have.

"As a deer pants for flowing streams, so pants my soul for you, O God."

The psalmist is not flourishing in this moment. He is not drawing from a reservoir of spiritual abundance accumulated in better seasons. His tears have been his food. Others have been asking him where his God is. And the question lands not just as an external taunt but as an interior wound, because part of him is asking it, too.

This is what unguarded grief sounds like when a person refuses to dress it up. The psalmist is not in a place of confident declaration. He is in a place of genuine longing — longing for the presence of God, the way a person who has gone too long without water longs for it. Not as a preference. As a need. As something without which the interior cannot sustain itself.

But watch what he does with that longing. He does not suppress it. He does not resolve it quickly with a theological answer or a decision to feel differently. He holds it, honestly, and then does something that is neither denial nor despair. He speaks to his own soul.

"Why are you cast down, O my soul, and why are you in turmoil within me? Hope in God; for I shall again praise him."

This is not performance. The psalmist is not pretending that the darkness is not real. He is not generating a positive emotion to replace the difficult one, as though the right spiritual technique could lift him above his circumstances by force of will. He is doing something more fundamental — he is redirecting the governing center of his interior. He is refusing to let his soul's current experience of God be the final account of who God is. He is reaching for the cord even when he cannot feel its tautness and insisting that the fixed point is still there.

The phrase I shall again praise him is a declaration about the future made from the middle of a present that does not feel like it leads there. It is hope operating as a structural conviction rather than an emotional state. The praise is not yet present. The felt nearness of God is not yet present. The resolution of the circumstances that produced the grief is not yet present. But the certainty that these things will return — held not as a feeling but as a governing orientation — is precisely what keeps the interior from fully collapsing while the dark season continues.

The refrain appears three times across Psalms 42 and 43. Why are you cast down, O my soul. Each repetition suggests that the redirection is not a single moment but a repeated act. The soul does not stay redirected by one declaration. It drifts back. It requires the redirection again. And again. Not as evidence of failure but as evidence of what sustained hope actually looks like in practice — not a permanent arrival at a state of settled peace, but a continuous returning to the fixed point, a repeated choosing of orientation when the orientation does not choose itself.

The soul that has been rebuilt around hope sounds like this—not perpetually elevated. Not untouched by difficulty. But refusing to let the difficulty have the governing word. Returning, again and again, to the character of the One who holds the fixed point. Choosing, in the absence of felt certainty, to orient toward what is known rather than what is felt. And finding, over time, that the choosing reshapes the feeling — that the cord, held consistently, gradually draws the interior back toward the source.

The Psalms do not describe people who never struggled. They describe people who never stopped turning toward God in the struggle.

Psalm 13 traces the same journey in compressed form. David opens with four iterations of the question "How long" — how long will you forget me, how long will you hide your face, how long must I take counsel in my own soul, how long will my enemy be exalted. The repetition is not a literary excess. It is the honest interior experience of prolonged suffering, in which the same question returns each day that does not bring the resolution hoped for.

But then, without any change in circumstances, something shifts. David moves from lament to petition: consider me, answer me, light up my eyes. And then, without any reported change in what is happening around him, he arrives at this:

"But I have trusted in your steadfast love; my heart shall rejoice in your salvation. I will sing to the Lord, because he has dealt bountifully with me."

The past tense of the trust, the future tense of the rejoicing, the present tense of the singing — all three are present simultaneously. What David experienced, what he expects, and what he chooses right now in the middle of the circumstances that have not yet changed — these are all anchored in the same thing: the steadfast love of God, which does not shift with circumstances because circumstances do not produce it. It is an attribute of God's character. And God's character is the fixed point to which the cord is attached.

Jeremiah is a different kind of hope witness than Job or the psalmists, because his hope was tested not by personal catastrophe but by decades of prophetic faithfulness that, from every visible angle, appeared to produce nothing.

He was called to deliver a message his people did not want to hear. Warning of coming judgment. Calls to repentance that fell on hardened ears. Prophecies of destruction that made him the most unwelcome voice in the city, then the most ridiculed, then the most actively persecuted. His own family rejected him. He was imprisoned. He was thrown into a cistern and left to sink in the mud. He was repeatedly told by false prophets that his message was wrong, and by the people he was trying to reach that he was a traitor for saying what he did.

And through all of it, he kept saying it. Not because he did not feel the cost. Jeremiah 20 contains one of the most painfully honest passages in

Scripture, in which the prophet essentially tells God that he feels deceived — that the calling he accepted has made him a laughingstock, that every time he speaks, he cries out violence and destruction, that the word of the Lord has become a reproach to him. He wishes he had never been born. He curses the day of his birth. He is not performing resilience. He is at the end of what he has.

And yet the very next verses reveal what the restored interior sounds like when it has truly found its anchor: there is in my heart, as it were, a burning fire shut up in my bones, and I am weary with holding it in, and I cannot. He tried to stop. He could not. The cord held even as he tried to cut it himself. The fixed point would not release him even in the season when he most wanted to be released.

This is not a comfortable portrait of hope. It does not look like confidence, clarity, or the serene trust of a person who has moved beyond struggle. It looks like a man who is simultaneously falling apart and refusing to give up — who is honest about the cost of his calling and incapable of abandoning it. That incapacity is not weakness. It is the evidence of a cord that runs deeper than feeling, deeper than circumstance, deeper even than the person's own desire to be released from the burden of carrying it.

From the outside, the entire ministry of Jeremiah appeared to be a failure. The nation did not turn. The judgment came. Jerusalem fell. The temple was destroyed. The people went into exile. Everything Jeremiah had given his life to prevent happened.

And yet Lamentations — written during or immediately after the destruction of the city Jeremiah had spent his entire life trying to protect — contains this:

"The steadfast love of the Lord never ceases; his mercies never come to an end; they are new every morning; great is your faithfulness. The Lord is my portion, says my soul, therefore I will hope in him."

Read that against its context. The city is in ruins. The temple is ash. The people are in chains, being marched to a foreign land. And Jeremiah is writing about mercies that are new every morning. Not because the morning looks good. Because the character of the God who made the morning does not change when the morning is terrible.

The therefore in that passage is doing enormous work. It is not saying that circumstances provide grounds for hope. It is saying that God's character — His steadfast love, His faithfulness, the simple irreducible fact of being His — provides grounds for hope regardless of what circumstances look like. The Lord is my portion. Not the outcome. Not the vindication of the prophetic calling. Not the rebuilt city or the returned people. God Himself. And a soul whose portion is God Himself has something that no external event can remove, because the thing it is holding cannot be taken by the things that take everything else.

The Lord is my portion, says my soul, therefore I will hope.

This is the deepest expression of what hope looks like in the restored interior. Not the hope that things will get better — though they often do. Not the hope that the effort will be vindicated before others, though sometimes it is. The hope that is anchored in the character of God so completely that it persists even when the outcomes that would seem to validate it are entirely absent. This is tikvah at its fullest expression — a cord attached not to a desired future but to the living God, whose faithfulness does not depend on whether the current chapter of the story looks like it is heading anywhere good.

There is a particular quality to how a person who has received this kind of hope moves through ordinary life. It is recognizable without being dramatic, present without being performed.

They are not shaken in the ways that used to shake them. The difficult conversation that once would have destabilized their interior for the rest of the day is carried differently. Not without feeling — they feel it fully. But the feeling passes through a settled interior rather than landing in a disordered one. The disruption is registered, not suppressed. It is felt at its actual weight, neither amplified by anxiety nor minimized by the effort to appear fine. And then it is released in a way that was not possible before, because the governing center is not organized around managing disruption. It is organized around something that disruption cannot reach.

They interpret God differently than they used to. In seasons of disorder, the soul misread God consistently — His silence as disinterest, His timing as neglect, His process as abandonment. The person whose hope has been rebuilt reads the same silences and the same delays through a different lens. Not through naive positivity or the practiced suppression of doubt. Through a governing trust in the character of the One to whom the cord is attached. They do not assume that unanswered prayer means unheard prayer. They do not conclude that difficulty means distance. The same experiences that once confirmed their fear now confirm their faith — not because the experiences changed, but because the interpretive framework that processes them has been rebuilt from a different foundation.

They carry a quality of settled expectation. The person in disorder either expects things to work out because they cannot tolerate the alternative, or stops expecting anything because expectation has become too costly and too frequently disappointed. The person whose hope has been restored expects God — not a specific outcome, not a particular timeline, but God Himself. Present in the ordinary day. Working in the circumstances that look like obstacles. Doing something in the waiting that the waiting itself is necessary for. That expectation is not wishful thinking. It is the natural orientation of an interior that has been rebuilt around the character of a God who has proven Himself faithful across every season the person has actually lived through — including the ones that looked nothing like faithfulness while they were happening.

A soul rebuilt around hope does not brace against the future. It leans toward it.

This expectation is also one of the most visible qualities of such a person to those around them. There is a groundedness that does not depend on favorable circumstances. They can be in the middle of a difficult season and still have something to offer the people around them — not because they are performing a strength they do not have, but because the source they are drawing from is not depleted by difficulty the way human reserves are. The cord runs to a fixed point that the difficulty cannot reach. And from that point, even in the hard season, something continues to flow.

This is what Paul was describing when he told the Corinthians that he was afflicted in every way but not crushed, perplexed but not driven to despair, persecuted but not forsaken, struck down but not destroyed. The affliction was real. The perplexity was real. The persecution was real. None of it was minimized or spiritually reinterpreted as something other than what it was. But none of it reached the governing center. The cord held. And the holding of it produced a quality of presence and endurance that Paul himself attributed not to his own character or his own spiritual maturity, but to the treasure being carried in an earthen vessel — the surpassing power belonging to God rather than to him.

That is what genuine hope restored looks like in a human life. Not immunity to difficulty. The capacity to carry difficulty from a center that difficulty cannot reorganize. Not the absence of dark seasons. The presence of a cord that holds through them — that holds, and holds, and holds, until the season that looked like it would be permanent reveals itself to be a chapter, and the next chapter begins.

Hope is always first in the sequence of what restoration produces because, without it, nothing else can be received.

Abundance cannot enter a soul that still expects lack. The lens of scarcity reads even genuine provision as insufficient — filters it before it reaches the interior, converts gifts into anxiety about whether they will last, and turns generosity into a question about what the giver wants in return.

The soul that has not yet had its hope restored cannot receive abundance, not because abundance is withheld, but because the interpretive framework through which it would be received is still shaped by fear. What God provides passes through a filter that distorts it before it can become what it was intended to be.

Virtue cannot grow in soil hardened by resignation. The moral coherence that restoration produces — character that holds across conditions rather than performing well in favorable ones and collapsing when conditions change — requires an interior that is not perpetually in survival mode. The soul that has concluded that certain things will never change does not have the interior stability that genuine character requires. It manages behavior rather than expressing character. And managed behavior, held in place by effort rather than flowing from a reordered interior, fails the moment the effort becomes unsustainable. Which it always eventually does.

Empowerment cannot rest on a soul still convinced that collapse is inevitable. The capacity to live with genuine forward influence rather than reactive survival requires a governing center that is not consumed by the anxiety of self-protection. The person who does not yet have hope — who is still bracing, still guarding, still waiting for the other shoe to drop — cannot receive the strength that flows through an aligned interior. The channel is not yet open. The interior architecture has not yet been prepared to carry what would otherwise be available to it.

Hope is what opens it. Hope softens the soil. Hope loosens fear's grip on the interpretive framework. Hope reopens the interior space that God will fill with what follows. It is not the destination. It is the doorway through which everything else enters. And it is always, without exception, what God restores first.

This is why every account of genuine restoration in Scripture begins here. Before the provision, the hope. Before the character, the hope. Before the empowerment, the hope. God does not pour abundance into a vessel still shaped by scarcity. He first rebuilds the vessel. He first restores its capacity to hold what He intends to give. He first reattaches the cord to the fixed point so that the interior has an anchor that the subsequent seasons — with all their demands, disruptions, and ordinary Mondays — cannot pull loose.

Hope is not the destination. It is the doorway through which everything else enters.

The person whose hope has been restored does not necessarily look different on the outside. They still face the same circumstances. They still carry the same responsibilities. The week is still the week, with all its demands, interruptions, and moments that require more than the person feels they have.

But something has shifted in how they face it.

The Monday morning that used to arrive with the weight of a returning separation — the clarity of Sunday already thinning, the demands of the week already assembled, the familiar sense of being slightly behind before the day has properly begun — that Monday morning is different now. Not transformed beyond recognition. Different in a way that is felt more than named. The weight is lighter. The distance between Sunday and

Monday feels less automatic. The interior that woke up is the same interior that went to sleep on Sunday, because the cord that ran to the fixed point during worship did not go slack when the worship ended and the week began.

The revelation received on Sunday does not require as much effort to carry into Monday. It does not slip through the fingers as quickly. It meets the first difficult conversation of the week not as something fragile that must be protected from reality, but as something structural built to sustain contact with reality. The soul that carries it has been rebuilt to hold it. The cord is taut. The fixed point is real. And the soul attached to it moves into the ordinary week not as someone who is already losing what they received, but as someone still connected to the source that gave it.

That continuity — small, quiet, easy to miss if you are looking for something dramatic — is the first evidence that the gap is closing. Not because Sunday was more intense. Because the interior carrying Sunday's revelation into Monday has been rebuilt to hold it.

That is hope. Not the emotion. The architecture.

The architecture that makes everything else that follows possible.

And it is always, always first.

Once hope has been restored — once the cord is taut and the soul has found its anchor again — the interior is prepared to receive what comes next.

But receiving it requires something the disordered soul could not do. It requires seeing what is actually there.

The enemy's first move in the garden was not to remove provision. It was to change the lens through which provision was seen. To make abundance look like restriction. To make a garden full of every tree into a world defined by the one tree that was off-limits.

That lens — the scarcity lens — has been governing the interior ever since. And until it is rebuilt, even a soul anchored by hope cannot fully receive what God has been providing all along.

That is what the next chapter addresses.

The shift from scarcity to abundance. The second piece of evidence that the gap is closing. And the second thing that was already in Adam's hands on the sixth day — before he had worked a single hour to earn it.

IX

Abundance: The Shift from Scarcity

"The thief comes only to steal and kill and destroy. I came that they may have life and have it abundantly." —John 10:10

On the sixth day, before Adam had planted a single seed, the garden was already full.

Every tree bearing fruit. Every river runs clear. Gold and precious stones in the earth beneath his feet — resources he had not mined and would not need to survive, placed there anyway because extravagance is how God builds. The provision was not waiting to be earned. It was not the reward for a good harvest or a faithful season. It was the starting condition. Abundance was the atmosphere Adam woke up in before his first day of work had ever begun.

That is the second thing God gave on Day 6.

Not optimism. Not the promise that things would eventually be enough. An environment of extravagant, unearned, unrestricted provision — surrounding the human being before a single act of stewardship had been performed.

And then the serpent arrived. And his first move — as we traced in Chapter 3 — was not to remove the provision. It was to change the lens through which the provision was seen. To shift the focus from every tree you may freely eat to the one tree you may not. Same garden. Same abundance. Completely different perception. In a single sentence, a world of extravagant provision became a world of restriction and withheld resources.

That lens — the scarcity lens — has been governing the interior ever since. And the H.A.V.E. Effect cannot be fully received by a soul that is still looking through it because a soul shaped by scarcity does not receive abundance when it arrives. It filters it. It converts a provision into anxiety about whether it will hold. It turns generosity into calculation. It reads God's timing as withholding and His process as delay.

The second movement of restoration is the rebuilding of that lens. Not the addition of more provision — the provision has always been there. The restoration of the interior framework through which provision is received. When that framework is rebuilt, the soul begins to see what has been surrounding it all along.

Scarcity does not announce itself as a belief.

It announces itself as a reflex. The stomach tightens when the unexpected bill arrives. The mental calculation that runs automatically when someone asks for your time. The way praise lands and then immediately slides into the question of whether it will last. The exhaustion of a generosity that always has a quiet asterisk attached to it — given, but tallied. Offered, but monitored. Shared, but with one eye on whether the giving has left enough.

Most believers who operate from scarcity are unaware they are doing so. They do not describe themselves as doubters of God's provision. They believe in His faithfulness in the abstract, affirm it on Sunday, and carry it as a doctrinal conviction without difficulty. But between the conviction and the lived interior, something intervenes. Some layer of accumulated experience that taught the soul, quietly and repeatedly, that what it has is not quite enough, that what it receives will not quite hold, that the gap between what God promises and what Monday delivers is the permanent condition of a faith-filled life rather than a sign that something in the interior has not yet been rebuilt.

The shift that alignment produces is not primarily a shift in circumstances. The bills do not immediately resolve. The demands do not decrease. The week does not get shorter or easier. What shifts is the interior lens through which it is all received. And when that lens shifts — genuinely, structurally, not as a discipline applied from the outside but as the natural expression of a rebuilt interior — everything it touches looks different.

The word abundance carries more weight in Scripture than the prosperity culture of recent decades has allowed.

Jesus' promise in John 10 — I came that they may have life and have it abundantly — was not primarily a promise about outcomes. It was a declaration about the nature of the life that aligns with God. A life characterized not by scarcity and survival but by fullness, purpose, and an overflow that has somewhere to go. The Greek word *perissos*, translated abundantly, means beyond measure, exceeding what is necessary, superabundant. Jesus was not promising that the believer would never face need. He was describing the quality of the interior from which the believer faces everything — a quality that is not diminished by difficulty because it does not come from circumstances. It comes from the source to which the soul is connected.

The fall introduced scarcity thinking into the human soul in the same moment it introduced disorder. Standing in a garden of extravagant provision — every tree bearing fruit, every need anticipated and met, the presence of God Himself available in the cool of the day — Adam and Eve looked at the one restriction. They concluded that what they had been given was not enough. That God was withholding something they needed. The provision surrounding them was insufficient because one tree remained off limits.

This is the precise shape of scarcity thinking. It is not primarily about the absence of provision. It is about the inability to see and receive the provision that is present because the interior has been trained to focus on the gap rather than on the gift. The enemy's first strategy was not to create a lack. It was to convince the soul that the abundance surrounding it was inadequate. To shift the governing focus from what had been given to what had been withheld. And once that shift happened, everything that followed became possible.

The tragedy is not that God's provision was insufficient. The garden was full. The provision was extravagant beyond any honest accounting. The tragedy is that the soul, convinced by a single well-timed suggestion that the provision had a gap in it, could no longer see what was actually there. The abundance was real. The scarcity was a lens. And the lens, once adopted, filtered everything that came after it.

This is the condition that persists east of Eden. Not genuine lack — though genuine lack exists and is real and must be named honestly. The deeper condition is a soul that has inherited a scarcity lens and carries it into circumstances where genuine provision exists, reading the provision through the filter and finding it insufficient, confirming with each filtered reading the conviction that the filter was correct all along.

Alignment does not simply add more provision to a soul that is still looking through a scarcity lens. It rebuilds the lens. It restructures the interpretive framework through which provision is received. And when the framework is rebuilt, the soul begins to see what has been there all along.

Scarcity is not primarily about what is absent. It is about the inability to receive what is present.

The person whose interior has been rebuilt around God's provision begins to see differently. Not because the circumstances are different. Because the interpretive framework has been rebuilt. They begin to notice what is present rather than cataloguing what is missing. They begin to receive good things as evidence of a faithful God rather than as anomalies that must be protected before they disappear. They begin to experience provision not as a relief from the baseline state of lack but as a confirmation of the baseline state of being held.

This shift is subtle enough that the person experiencing it often cannot name it precisely. They notice it in the way the same bank account feels different. The same income that used to provoke anxiety about what might not be enough now inspires gratitude for what is present. The same schedule that used to feel like a constant deficit of time begins to feel like a set of choices about where to invest what has been given. The same relationships that used to feel like demands on a depleted reserve begin to feel like connections that add rather than cost.

The circumstances did not change. The interior changed. And a changed interior reads the same set of circumstances as a fundamentally different story.

Abraham understood provision before he had seen most of what God had promised him.

When conflict arose between his herdsmen and Lot's over grazing rights, Abraham had every reasonable claim to assert priority. He was the elder. The original covenant was with him. He could have assessed the situation, calculated his needs, and ensured his own interests were protected before offering anything to Lot. This is what the soul operating from scarcity does — it secures itself first and distributes from whatever remains.

Instead, Abraham offered Lot the choice. Take the left or the right. Whatever you want, I will take what is left. The whole land is before you.

This was not naïveté. Abraham had real herds, real herdsmen, and real competition for limited grazing land. He understood exactly what he was doing. What made the offer possible was not ignorance of the stakes but a governing conviction that his provision did not depend on which territory he ended up with. God had already spoken to him. God had already made promises to him. The land was not the source of his security. The God who gave the land was the source of his security. And the God who gave the land could provide just as well from the territory Lot did not want as from the territory Lot chose.

God's response was immediate. After Lot separated, God told Abraham to lift his eyes in every direction — north, south, east, west — and look at all the land He would give him and his offspring forever. The generosity that flowed from abundance thinking was met with the enlargement of the very thing Abraham had been willing to release his grip on.

This is not a formula. Generosity is not a technique for receiving more. But it is a consistent pattern in Scripture — the soul that holds loosely what it has been given, trusting in the character of the Giver rather than the security of the gift, repeatedly discovers that the Giver is more than capable of replenishing what was released.

The open hand receives what the closed hand cannot.

Abraham's generosity reappears throughout his story because abundance thinking is not a single decision. It is a governing orientation that expresses itself in situation after situation, each one a fresh opportunity to either grip tightly or hold loosely.

When three strangers appeared at his tent in the heat of the day, Abraham ran to meet them. He did not walk out cautiously to assess whether hospitality was warranted. He ran. And then he promised a little bread and water — modest language for what he actually prepared, which was the finest flour Sarah could bake into cakes, the best calf from the herd, tender and good, curds and milk alongside. He promised a morsel and produced a feast.

The contrast between the modest offer and the extravagant provision is significant. The soul operating from genuine trust in God's provision does not give from a carefully guarded minimum. It gives from overflow. Not because it does not know the cost, but because the cost is held lightly against the backdrop of a provision that the soul has learned to trust. Abraham was not performing generosity. He was expressing what an interior organized around God's abundance naturally produces when an opportunity presents itself.

The promise those strangers carried — that Sarah, well past the age of childbearing, would have a son within the year — arrived in the context of that hospitality. The generosity and the promise are connected in the text. Not as a transaction. But as a correlation. The soul that is genuinely oriented toward abundance is positioned to receive what the soul gripping its resources cannot.

Jesus encountered apparent scarcity repeatedly in His ministry and consistently responded in ways that reframed the governing question.

The feeding of five thousand men — along with women and children, likely bringing the crowd to fifteen or twenty thousand — from five loaves of bread and two fish is among the most recognizable miracles in the gospels. It is also one of the clearest pictures available of what abundance thinking looks like when it encounters genuine need and genuinely insufficient resources.

The disciples' response was entirely reasonable. It was late. The location was remote. The crowd was enormous. Send them away to buy food in the villages. This is the soul operating from a clear-eyed assessment of available resources and drawing the only logical conclusion: what is here is insufficient for what is needed; therefore, the need must go somewhere else. The disciples were not being faithless. They were being accurate. Five loaves and two fish cannot feed twenty thousand people. That is simply true.

Jesus' response reframed the entire situation. You give them something to eat. Not because the resources were adequate — they were obviously not. But because the adequacy of the resources was not the governing question. The governing question was what could happen when five loaves and two fish were placed in the hands of the One through whom everything that exists came into being.

He took what was brought, looked to heaven, gave thanks, broke it, and gave it back to the disciples to distribute. And somewhere between the breaking and the distributing, a crowd of thousands was fed, and twelve baskets of fragments remained—more at the end than at the beginning.

The disciples were right that five loaves and two fish were not enough to feed five thousand people. What they had not yet learned was that the arithmetic of the Kingdom operates differently from the arithmetic of scarcity. That which is insufficient in human hands is not insufficient when it is genuinely offered to the One who owns everything. The first move in every situation of apparent lack is not to calculate what is present against what is needed but to place what is present in hands that are not limited by human calculation.

This pattern recurs throughout both Testaments. The widow of Zarephath's jar of oil and handful of flour — offered to Elijah first, before her own need was met — did not run out for the duration of the drought. The widow in 2 Kings, with her jar of oil — the only asset she had to prevent her sons from being sold to pay her husband's debts — watched it fill every vessel she could find and then stop when the vessels were full. Not before. Not after. Exactly when the need was met.

The pattern is not that God multiplies for everyone who asks. It is the soul that has learned to bring what it has — honestly, without inflation, without pretending to have more than it does— and place it in open hands, tends to discover that what was genuinely insufficient was not the final word on what was available.

The soul that brings what it has — honestly, without performance — tends to discover that what was insufficient was not the final word.

Paul wrote about contentment as one of the clearest evidences of a soul that has learned to operate from abundance rather than scarcity. The passage is among the most quoted in the New Testament, and among the most misunderstood.

"I have learned, in whatever state I am, to be content. I know how to be brought low, and I know how to abound. In any and every circumstance, I have learned the secret of facing plenty and hunger, abundance and need."

The word learned is doing critical work there. Contentment is not a natural state. It is not the disposition of a person who has been given everything they need and therefore has nothing to be anxious about. It is a learned orientation — acquired through experience, through the repeated testing of a governing conviction against actual circumstances that pressed against it with full force.

Paul had been in both states. He knew abundance — the seasons when provision was generous, and the work was fruitful, and the churches were growing, and the support was coming in. And he knew want — the seasons of imprisonment, shipwreck, beatings, cold, hunger, the sense of abandonment by people he had poured himself into. He was not writing from a place of comfortable theology. He was writing from a place of tested experience. And what the testing had produced was not stoicism — the resigned acceptance of whatever comes. It was something more interior than that. The settled orientation of a soul that had found its source and discovered that the source did not change when the circumstances did.

"I can do all things through him who strengthens me."

This line is often quoted as a motivational declaration. In context, it is something more specific and more honest. It is the declaration of a man who has learned that his capacity is not determined by his circumstances but by his connection to the One who holds him. In abundance, he does not grasp. In want, he does not collapse. Because neither abundance nor want is the governing condition. The governing condition is the source. And the source does not change.

This is what contentment looks like in the interior of a person whose alignment has been restored. Not the absence of preference or desire. Not the performance of happiness with whatever is present. The genuine, experientially acquired conviction that what they have is enough because the One who gave it is faithful — and that whether more arrives or less, the governing reality remains the same.

Contentment is not the absence of desire. It is the presence of a source that remains constant even when circumstances change.

The soul that has learned this reads provision differently than the soul that has not. When provision is generous, it does not produce the anxious question of whether it will last. It produces gratitude — genuine, undefended gratitude that receives the gift as the expression of a character rather than as luck that may not hold. When provision is lean, it does not lead to a collapse in confidence in God's care. It produces the settled, sometimes uncomfortable, but ultimately stable trust that the same character that was provided in the generous season is present in the lean one.

Both responses — gratitude in abundance, trust in want — are the fruit of the same interior restructuring. They are not performed. They are the natural expression of a soul that has been reordered around a source that does not vary with seasons. And the soul that has been rebuilt to carry both is one that the week, with all its fluctuations, cannot reorganize.

Generosity is the most visible evidence of a soul that has genuinely shifted from scarcity to abundance. Not generosity as spiritual discipline

— the measured giving that fulfills an obligation or maintains a standing. Generosity as overflow. The natural, almost unrehearsed expression of an interior that has received so much it cannot hold it all.

The Macedonian churches that Paul described to the Corinthians were experiencing severe affliction and extreme poverty. These are not metaphors. The churches in Macedonia were under real pressure — financial, relational, and likely physical. By every external calculation, they were the last people who should have been giving anything to the Jerusalem relief fund. They had nothing to spare.

And yet Paul describes their giving as an abundance of joy overflowing in a wealth of generosity. They gave beyond their means. They begged Paul for the privilege of participating in the offering. They did not give reluctantly, after careful calculation of what they could technically afford. They gave from a conviction so deep about what they had received in the Messiah that the material poverty surrounding them could not govern the interior orientation from which the giving flowed.

Paul identifies the source clearly: they gave themselves first to the Lord and then, by the will of God, to the apostles. The material generosity was the overflow of an interior surrender. The giving of money followed a prior giving of self. The soul that has genuinely placed itself in God's hands does not experience material generosity as a cost. It experiences it as the natural expression of who it has become.

This is what generosity looks like when it is genuinely free. Not the performance of openhandedness for the sake of reputation or the calculated giving that expects a visible return. The unrehearsed, undefended, sometimes slightly illogical giving of someone who has discovered that what they have does not actually belong to them in the way they thought. That they are stewards, not owners. That the resources passing through their hands are meant to flow, not accumulate. That the closed hand does not protect what it holds — it only prevents it from becoming what it was meant to be.

Generosity is not a discipline the aligned soul imposes on itself. It is the overflow of a soul that has been rebuilt around abundance.

The widow in Mark 12 gave two small coins into the temple treasury — the smallest currency in use, less than a penny in any modern equivalent. Everyone else that day gave larger amounts. Some gave conspicuously large amounts. Jesus watched it all from across the court and said nothing.

Then He called His disciples over and pointed to the widow. This woman, He said, has given more than all the others. Because all of them gave up their surplus, she had to give up everything she had to live on.

The measure of generosity in the Kingdom is not the amount given against an absolute standard. It is the amount given against what was available to give. The widow's two coins represented a ratio that the large gifts of the wealthy contributors did not approach. She gave everything. They gave from excess. Her giving cost her everything she had. It cost them the discomfort of appearing slightly less wealthy than they were.

What the widow had that the others did not was not a greater capacity for sacrifice. It was a governing conviction about the source of her security. She was not holding onto those two coins as her final insurance against a God who might not provide. She was releasing them as the expression of a trust that had already moved beyond what the coins represented. Her security was not in the coins. It was in the One to whom she was returning them.

That conviction — held not as a theological idea but as a governing reality that determined what she actually did with the last of what she had — is the shape of abundance thinking at its most refined. It is not the result of having nothing to lose. It is the result of having found the One thing that cannot be lost, and organizing everything else around that.

The abundant life that alignment produces does not look like unlimited resources. It does not look like immunity from financial pressure or release from the ordinary constraints of a life lived inside real economic conditions. What it looks like is something more interior and more durable than any of those things.

It looks like a person who is genuinely free with what they have.

Free in the sense that the resources they carry — money, time, attention, capacity, knowledge, connection — are not gripped. They are held in open hands, ready to move when the need presents itself, ready to be given when the moment calls for it, ready to be invested in something larger than self-protection when the opportunity arises. Not because the person is naïve about need or indifferent to prudent stewardship. Because the governing question has shifted from 'how do I protect what I have?' to 'what is this meant to accomplish?'

It looks like a person who receives good things well. Who does not immediately convert a gift into anxiety about whether it will last. Who can sit in a season of genuine provision and let it be what it is — evidence of a faithful God, not a fragile anomaly that must be protected before it disappears. Who gives thanks without the asterisk of worry. Who enjoys what is present without being haunted by what might not always be.

It looks like a person who does not need to accumulate proof of God's faithfulness before trusting Him with the next thing. They already know who He is. They have learned it — not as doctrine but as lived experience, through seasons that tested the conviction and found it reliable. The next season, whatever it brings, will be met by an interior that is not starting from scratch.

The abundant life is not the life of unlimited resources. It is the life of a soul no longer governed by the fear of not enough.

This freedom expresses itself in the smallest things as readily as in the large ones. The person whose interior has been rebuilt around abundance does not keep a mental ledger of what they have given and what they are owed. They do not experience the dinner table as a transaction or the mentoring conversation as a withdrawal from a reserve that needs replenishing before more can be offered. They give attention without calculating the return. They offer time without checking the balance. Not because they have infinite capacity — they do not. But because the governing question is not whether the capacity is infinite. It is whether the Person who sustains the capacity is faithful. And on that question, the evidence has been sufficient.

They are also free to receive. This is less obvious but equally significant. The soul that operates from scarcity not only struggles to give. It struggles to receive. To let provision be provision. To accept help without immediately converting it into a debt. To be cared for without the discomfort of dependence on something outside itself. The soul organized around abundance can receive as freely as it gives, because receiving is simply another form of acknowledging that all of it comes from God. The gift from the friend and the gift from the field both flow from the same source. The open hand holds both.

There is a particular quality in the way a person who has genuinely shifted from scarcity to abundance carries their own calling and the work of their life.

The soul in scarcity relates to calling with a quality of urgency that has anxiety underneath it. The work must succeed because the soul's sense of security is partially organized around its success. The gifts must be recognized, because the soul's sense of worth is partially organized around being seen. The effort must bear fruit because the soul's confidence in being in right standing with God is partially organized around visible results. None of this is conscious or deliberate. It is the natural expression of a soul that has not yet found its security in the right place. And it produces a quality of driven effort that can look like faith from a distance but is often closer to fear.

The soul that has genuinely moved into abundance relates to calling differently. The work is done with full effort — more full effort, often, than the anxious soul produces, because effort is no longer being siphoned off by the background hum of self-protection. But the effort is not gripping. The outcome is held in open hands. The fruit is received with gratitude when it comes and with trust when it does not, because the soul's security is not organized around the outcome. It is organized around the One who assigned the work.

This produces a quality of steadiness in the middle of circumstances that would otherwise destabilize. The project that stalls. The relationship does not develop as hoped. The season in which the work seems to be producing nothing visible. The person whose interior is organized around abundance does not read these circumstances as evidence of divine abandonment or personal inadequacy. They read them as the normal texture of a life lived by faith rather than by sight.

They bring the five loaves and the two fish. They give thanks. They distribute what they have. And they trust the arithmetic to the One whose arithmetic has never ultimately failed.

That trust — not as a feeling but as a governing orientation, held through the ordinary week with all its fluctuations and demands and moments when the visible evidence is insufficient — is the fruit that abundance produces in the life that has been genuinely restructured around it. It is not spectacular. It does not announce itself. But it is deeply, durably present.

And in the moments when the soul either grips or releases, it is the difference between a life consumed by what it fears it does not have and a life sustained by what it knows it has been given.

That is abundance. Not the amount in the account. The orientation of the interior.

And when the interior has been rebuilt, the account — whatever it holds — is enough.

Hope reattaches the cord. Abundance rebuilds the lens.

Together they begin to produce something that the disordered interior could not sustain — not through effort, not through discipline, not through the managed performance of a person trying to hold their life together from the outside in.

They begin to produce character.

Not the behavior a person performs when they are being watched. Not the consistency maintained through sufficient effort in favorable conditions. Character that holds. The same on every surface. Present under pressure in the same form it is present in ease.

This is the third thing Adam had on Day 6 before his first Monday existed. Not a discipline to develop. An expression of the design he was carrying — naked and unashamed, with nothing to perform and nothing to hide, the interior and the exterior a single coherent life.

That is what the next chapter describes.

X

Virtue: Character That Holds

"Have this mind among yourselves, which is yours in Christ Jesus, who, though he was in the form of God, did not count equality with God a thing to be grasped, but emptied himself, by taking the form of a servant." —
Philippians 2:5-7

On the sixth day, Adam and Eve were naked and unashamed.

Not because they had achieved a level of spiritual maturity where self-exposure no longer felt dangerous. Not because they had worked through every wound and resolved every vulnerability. But because nothing in them was misaligned. The interior and the exterior were a single coherent life. There was no gap between who they were and who they appeared to be. No Sunday version is being maintained for public consumption, while a different version is operated in private. No energy is spent on managing perception—no distance between what was known about them and what was shown.

That is the original form of virtue.

Not a discipline imposed from outside. Not behavior held in acceptable shape by the effort of will. The natural, uncontrived expression of an interior that had nothing to perform and nothing to hide — because the architecture was intact, the sequence was ordered, and the soul was operating from the design it was built for.

When disorder entered, that integration shattered. The first thing Adam and Eve did after the fall was reach for coverings. Not because the physical reality had changed. Because the interior had. The gap between who they were and who they appeared to be opened in an instant, and the instinct to manage it — to present one version while protecting another — arrived with it. That instinct has been running in every human soul ever since.

The third movement of the H.A.V.E. Effect is the restoration of that integration. Virtue — not as a standard to be reached, but as the natural expression of a soul that has been rebuilt from the inside out. A character that holds not because it is being held together by effort, but because the interior has been reordered around a foundation that does not require the gap.

When hope has been restored and the abundance lens has been rebuilt, the soul stops spending its energy on managing scarcity and on the anxiety of self-protection. That freed energy does not simply disappear. It becomes the raw material of character. The soul that is no longer gripping has something to give. The soul that is no longer hiding has something to show. And what it shows — gradually, over the ordinary days of an ordinary life — is who it is actually becoming.

Character is not what you do when people are watching.

That is the common definition, and it is not wrong, but it is incomplete. Character is what you do when no one is watching, and the pressure to appear a certain way has been removed. But more than that, character is what happens automatically. What comes out when something squeezes you unexpectedly? What surfaces before you have time to choose the better version of yourself? The reaction before the reflection.

What most people experience in that unguarded moment is not who they want to be. It is who the interior has been shaped to be by years of accumulated patterns, pressures, and compensations. The sharpness that surfaces under stress. The defensiveness that arrives before the conversation has a chance to go anywhere. The smallness that tightens around recognition when someone else receives it first. These are not character failures in the moment. They are the interior's honest report on what has been governing it.

This is why alignment matters for virtue. The aligned life does not produce good character by requiring more effort. It produces good character by rebuilding the interior from which character flows. The virtue that emerges from a restored soul is not managed behavior — behavior held in acceptable shape by the effort of will. It is expressed character. The natural, consistent, largely effortless expression of who the interior has actually become.

This distinction is everything. Managed behavior is exhausting and brittle. It holds under normal conditions and breaks under real pressure. Expressed character holds under pressure precisely because it is not being held at all. It is simply what the interior produces when squeezed.

The Hebrew concept embedded in the word *tamim* — usually translated as " blameless or integrity — carries an architectural meaning that the English word loses. Tamim means complete. Whole. Without missing parts. The same on every surface. When the word is applied to a person, it describes not moral perfection but interior coherence — the quality of being the same person across conditions. The same in the marketplace as in the prayer room. The same under pressure as in ease. The same applies whether the outcome is uncertain or secure.

This is what the restored interior produces. Not a person who never struggles or never sins. A person who is no longer divided against themselves. Who does not have a public self and a private self operating on different principles. Who does not need to manage the gap between what they present and what they actually are, because the gap has narrowed to the point where management is no longer required.

Most of the exhaustion that believers carry is not the exhaustion of doing too much. It is the exhaustion of internal division — of maintaining a version of themselves for one context that is different from the version required for another, of keeping all the plates of self-presentation spinning simultaneously, of living in the gap between who they appear to be and who the interior actually is. The aligned soul does not carry this exhaustion. Not because it has no weakness. Because it is no longer managing the gap. What it is on the inside is close enough to what it presents on the outside that the management work has largely dissolved.

Virtue is not the result of trying harder. It is the fruit of an interior rebuilt from the source.

Daniel is the clearest Old Testament portrait of what this kind of character looks like operating inside a system specifically designed to unmake it.

He was taken from Jerusalem as a teenager — stripped of his homeland, his community, his name, and every external marker of identity that had structured his sense of self and placed inside the Babylonian court, which was designed not just to employ him but to remake him — to replace his governing framework with one organized around Babylonian values, Babylonian gods, and Babylonian definitions of success and security.

The king's food was the first test. Not obviously dramatic. Not a direct command to bow before an idol. Just the ordinary provision of the court — the same food everyone else ate, the food that signaled participation in the culture and acceptance of its terms. Daniel resolved that he would not defile himself with it. Not with visible heroics or public declaration. Quietly, firmly, and with a proposed alternative that gave the official an honorable way to accommodate the request.

The text says Daniel resolved. The Hebrew word carries the sense of setting something in the heart — a prior governing decision that precedes the specific situation rather than being made inside it. Daniel was not deciding in the moment whether this mattered enough to risk his position over. He had already decided, at a level deeper than circumstance, who he was and what his life was organized around. The specific situation only revealed what had already been settled.

This is the shape of character produced by an aligned interior. The decision is not made fresh in each new situation, under the pressure of that situation's particular stakes. It has already been made at the governing center level. The situation surfaces what is already there. Which is why, across decades in Babylon — across changes of regime, shifts in political fortune, rivals who tried to find fault in him, laws designed specifically to trap him — Daniel's character remained consistent. Not because he was trying harder in each new crisis. Because the interior that met each new crisis was the same interior that had met all the previous ones, and it had already settled the governing question.

The officials who investigated him found no charges or fault because he was faithful, and no error or fault was found in him. That is *tamim*. Not perfect. Consistent. The same person in the court records as in the prayer room. The same person was favored by the king, as when the king forgot him. The same person in the lions' den as in the throne room. A character that held not because the conditions were favorable but because the interior had been organized around something that conditions could not reach.

Virtue in the ordinary life of a believer is not primarily tested in dramatic moments of moral crisis. It is tested in the ten thousand small moments that make up the average week. The email that requires a response to someone who has been dismissive. The meeting where credit is distributed in ways that do not reflect the actual contributions made. The conversation with the family member whose choices you find exhausting and whose pattern you have named to yourself many times before. The moment when the impulse to take a shortcut presents itself in a way that is entirely defensible.

These are the real tests of character. Not because they are more important than the dramatic ones — the dramatic ones carry their own weight. But because they happen constantly, because they happen when no one is particularly watching or evaluating, and because the habit of response that is built in the small moments is exactly the habit that will surface in the large ones.

The soul that has been rebuilt around God's provision does not need to perform goodness in these moments. It does not need to summon the will to respond with patience rather than sharpness, with honesty rather than impression management, with care for the other person rather than care for its own reputation. These responses are available because the interior has been restructured around something that does not require the moment's pressure to be the governing factor.

Paul described this to the Philippians from a Roman prison, which is a relevant context for everything he wrote about character. He was not writing from a position of comfort or control. He was writing from a position in which his circumstances were entirely outside his management and in which the quality of his interior life had become the only thing that was genuinely his. And he wrote about contentment as something learned. About peace as something that passes understanding. About the ability to think on whatever is true and honorable and just and pure and lovely and commendable as a choice available to a mind that has been anchored to a different governing center than the circumstances pressing in on it from every side.

The peace Paul described is not the peace of resolved circumstances. It is the peace of a soul that has found its anchor and is no longer being reorganized by the weather. The character that flows from that peace — the gentleness, the reasonableness, the capacity to be present to others without being depleted by them — is not manufactured by effort. It is what a soul at peace naturally expresses.

---

*The character that flows from peace is not
manufactured by effort. It is what a soul at peace
naturally expresses.*

Virtue in the marketplace is one of the most visible and most practically significant expressions of the aligned life.

For most believers, the majority of their waking hours are spent in some form of work — professional employment, entrepreneurship, the labor of building and maintaining a household, the endless texture of practical responsibility that fills the ordinary week. This is not the margin of the life of faith. It is the primary arena in which a character either holds or does not. And it is the arena that many believers have quietly concluded is too secular to be significantly shaped by the interior work of alignment.

This conclusion is not supported by Scripture. The parable of the talents is set entirely in a marketplace context. The master distributes capital, assigns responsibility, leaves on a journey, and returns to evaluate what was done with what was given. The commendation — well done, good and faithful servant — is given not for prayer or worship or explicitly religious activity but for faithful, productive, fruit-bearing engagement with the work that was assigned. The marketplace is not where faith goes to take a break. It is where faith is demonstrated.

Daniel understood this. His distinctiveness in the Babylonian court was not primarily expressed in his private prayer life, though the prayer life was real and costly. It was expressed in the quality of his work. The officials who sought to find fault in him were not examining his theology. They were examining the king's conduct of the affairs. And they could find nothing — no negligence, no corruption, no inconsistency between what he reported and what was actually true. His faith and his work were not separate compartments. The interior that was organized around God's character expressed that organization in every dimension of his professional life.

An excellent spirit was in him. That is the text's explanation for why he was distinguished above all the other officials. Not superior intelligence, though he likely had it. Not political acumen, though he had that too. An excellent spirit. The interior quality that produced the exterior distinction. The alignment of the soul expressing itself in the excellence of the work.

This is what virtue in the marketplace actually looks like. Not the performance of Christian behavior as a separate layer added to professional competence. The expression of an interior that has been governed by integrity, faithfulness, and the conviction that the work is being done as unto God rather than as unto the watching evaluation of human managers. The person whose soul is organized this way does not need to decide freshly in each situation whether to cut corners or hold the standard. The standard is already settled. The question is only what the standard requires in this specific situation.

The marketplace is not where faith goes to take a break.
It is where faith is demonstrated.

Esther's story adds a dimension to virtue in the arena of institutional power that Daniel's story does not fully develop. She was not primarily an administrator or a practitioner of professional excellence. She was a person navigating a system in which her survival depended on her ability to be what the system required of her, while simultaneously being called to act in a way that the system would have condemned.

The virtue that Esther expressed when she chose to go to the king unsummoned was not primarily courage in the conventional sense, though it required courage. It was the virtue of a person who had found something more important than her own security to organize her choices around. Mordecai's challenge went to the heart of it: perhaps you have come to the kingdom for such a time as this. The question was whether her position was a privilege to protect or a resource to deploy. Whether her access to the king was for her security or as an assignment.

The soul organized around its own security answers that question one way. The soul that has been organized around something larger than self-protection answers it differently. Esther's response — if I perish, I perish — is not fatalism. It is the declaration of a person who has already settled the governing question. Her life was not the most important thing she was carrying. The people she was positioned to protect were. And that prior settlement made the specific decision, as terrifying as it was, available to her in a way it would not have been to a soul whose governing center was organized around self-preservation.

Virtue in the institutional arena always eventually arrives at this question. Not in the form of a single dramatic moment for most people — most people are not called to risk execution for their community. But in the smaller, repeated form of choices about whether a position is something to protect or something to steward. Whether access and influence are personal assets or responsibilities that carry obligations toward the people they could serve. The soul that has been rebuilt around abundance thinks differently about this than the soul organized around scarcity. And the difference expresses itself in the ordinary choices of every professional week, long before it surfaces in any moment of visible crisis.

Relationships are where virtue is most honestly revealed.

Not because relationships are the only arena that matters — the marketplace and the prayer room both matter. But relationships have a particular capacity to expose the actual condition of the interior by requiring sustained, unscripted contact with other human beings who are themselves complex, inconsistent, and frequently disappointing. The spiritual life can be curated in private. Relationships cannot be curated. They happen in real time, with real people, under conditions that the soul did not fully prepare for, and they surface what is actually governing the interior with a clarity that no amount of private discipline can replicate.

Paul's extended description of love in 1 Corinthians 13 is not primarily a description of romantic feeling or even of warm affection. It is a description of character under relational pressure. Love is patient — when the person in front of you is slow, frustrating, or failing to become who you can see they could be. Love is kind — when the same situation would justify sharpness or withdrawal. Love does not insist on its own way — when the soul's preference is strong, and the cost of yielding is real. Love bears all things, believes all things, hopes all things, endures all things — not as a feeling that arrives spontaneously, but as a governing orientation that holds even when the feeling has long since left.

This kind of love is not possible from a soul that is still operating from scarcity. The soul in scarcity experiences relationships primarily as a context in which its needs are either met or unmet, its security is either confirmed or threatened, and its investment is either returned or wasted. It keeps a ledger. Not consciously, not deliberately — but the ledger is kept, and when the balance tips too far in the wrong direction, the soul begins its withdrawal. This is not a failure of will. It is the natural expression of an interior organized around protecting itself from further loss.

The soul that has been rebuilt around God's provision relates to people differently. Not because it has eliminated preference or become indifferent to how relationships go. But because its security is no longer organized around how relationships go. It can be fully present to another person without needing that person's response to be a particular thing. It can love without the transaction. It can give without the ledger. Not infinitely — the restored soul still has limits and still needs the rhythms of renewal that keep it from genuine depletion. But the limit is real capacity, not the defensive management of a soul that is afraid to give what it has because it is not sure there will be more.

The soul rebuilt around abundance can love without
the transaction and give without the ledger.

Forgiveness is perhaps the most demanding expression of relational virtue because it requires releasing a legitimate claim. The person who was genuinely wronged has a genuine grievance. The hurt is real. The loss is real. The justice being sought is not unreasonable. And forgiveness does not deny any of this. It does not require the person to pretend that what happened did not happen or did not matter. It requires them to release the claim—to stop organizing the present around the debt the past created.

The soul operating from scarcity cannot do this easily. To release the claim feels like absorbing a loss it can barely afford. It means that the wrong will not be balanced by an equal wrong returned. It means that the person who cost the soul something will not be required to repay it. And to a soul that is already experiencing the interior world as a system of scarce resources and precarious balances, this feels like a cost it cannot sustain.

The soul operating from abundance forgives from a different place. Not because it does not feel wrong — it feels it fully. But because its sense of what it has and what it can afford is organized around a different source. It has received, from God, a mercy so disproportionate to what it deserved that the gap between what was taken from it and what it is releasing is not the governing calculation. The one who has been forgiven much loves much. The one who has received an abundance of grace can afford to distribute it without keeping careful records of the distribution.

This is not a demand. It is a description. The soul that has genuinely received the grace it has been given does not experience forgiveness as an expensive sacrifice. It experiences it as the natural expression of what has been poured into it. The overflow that abundance produces flows in the direction of the people the soul is in relationship with. Freely received, freely given, not as a discipline imposed from the outside, but as the organic expression of an interior that has been rebuilt around the character of the One who forgave first.

There is a quality to the person of genuine virtue that is recognizable in the texture of ordinary interaction, long before it is tested in any significant crisis.

They are consistent. Not in the sense of being predictable or without range — consistent people can be deeply complex and capable of a significant variety of expression. But consistent in the sense that the person you encounter in one context is recognizably the same person you encounter in another. The version they bring to the difficult conversation is not dramatically different from the version they bring to the easy one. The version that shows up when they are tired and pressed is not a stranger to the version that shows up when they are rested and resourced. What you see is reliably connected to what is actually there. The gap between presentation and interior is narrow enough that navigation between the two is not a significant feature of the relationship between them.

They are present. Not distracted by the performance of being present — not monitoring how their presence is landing or what impression it is creating. Actually present. The conversation they are in is the one they are attending to. The person in front of them is the one they are seeing. Not managing. Not positioning. Seeing. This quality of genuine presence is rare enough that people notice it without being able to name it precisely. They leave the conversation feeling genuinely heard rather than efficiently processed, which is a different experience and one that most people are hungry for.

They are stable without being rigid. The soul organized around a fixed point can be moved without being reorganized. Difficult news arrives and is received at its actual weight, without amplification through anxiety or minimization through the need to appear unaffected. The conversation takes an unexpected turn and is met with genuine responsiveness rather than defensive redirection. The plan changes, and the change is accommodated without the change becoming a crisis. Stability, in the aligned soul, is not the absence of movement. It is the presence of a governing center that movement cannot permanently displace.

These qualities — consistency, presence, stability — are not the product of personality. Some personalities tend in these directions more naturally than others. But genuine virtue is not the amplification of natural personality. It is the expression of a rebuilt interior, which means it is available to every personality type, and it is recognizably different from natural disposition in the degree to which it holds under pressure. The naturally warm person becomes warmer in the best conditions and withdraws in the difficult ones. The person of genuine virtue is warm in the best conditions and still genuinely present in the difficult ones. The difference is not personality. It is the interior from which the warmth flows.

The fruit of the Spirit that Paul describes in Galatians 5 is not a list of disciplines to pursue. It is a description of what the Spirit produces in a life that has been genuinely surrendered to His governance.

Love, joy, peace, patience, kindness, goodness, faithfulness, gentleness, self-control. The word fruit is singular in the original — not fruits, as though they are nine separate items to be acquired one at a time. One fruit with nine expressions—the single harvest of a single surrender to a single source.

This matters for how the person of genuinely aligned character experiences their own virtue. They do not experience it as the achievement of nine separate qualities through nine separate efforts. They experience it as the natural overflow of an interior that has been rebuilt around the character of God. Patience is not a discipline imposed on an impatient soul by force of will. It is the expression of a soul that has received so much patience from God that it has some to give. The kindness is not performed. It is the natural behavior of an interior organized around the character of the One who is kind. The peace is not managed. It is the settled condition of a soul that has found its anchor and is no longer being swept by every current.

This does not mean virtue is effortless or that the aligned soul never struggles. The process of alignment is ongoing. The interior continues to be shaped and reshaped across the seasons of life. There are areas where the fruit is ripe and areas where it is still forming. There are days when the peace holds easily, and days when holding it requires actively redirecting the governing center back to its source. The honest account of a virtuous life is not a life without struggle. It is a life in which the struggle is increasingly with what is genuinely difficult rather than with the management of an interior that is divided against itself.

Virtue is the single harvest of a single surrender to a single source.

The person in whom this kind of character is forming does not announce it. A character that announces itself is not yet fully formed. The genuinely virtuous soul is not managing its reputation for virtue — it is simply being what it is and allowing the expression of that to speak for itself over time. Daniel did not promote his own integrity. The people who needed to see it saw it. Esther did not publicize her courage. The act itself was the declaration. The Macedonian churches did not advertise their generosity. Paul reported it afterward, to others, as evidence of what the Spirit produces in surrendered lives.

This is the final mark of genuine virtue. It does not need an audience. It does not require external validation to sustain itself. It is not diminished by the absence of recognition or inflated by its presence. It simply is — the consistent, quiet, durable expression of an interior that has been rebuilt around something that recognition cannot improve and neglect cannot erode.

That is a character that holds. Not because the person is extraordinary. Because the source is.

Hope. Abundance. Virtue.

Three of the four things Adam had on the sixth day before his first Monday had ever existed. The cord is attached to the fixed point. The lens that received provision without filtering it through fear. The integrity of a life with nothing to perform and nothing to hide.

Each one is real. Each one is the natural expression of a rebuilt interior. Each one is evidence that the gap is closing.

But there is a fourth.

The one that takes everything the first three have produced — the anchored soul, the open hand, the integrated life — and makes it available to the world around it. Not as a performance. Not as a strategy. As the overflow of a life that has been genuinely returned to its source.

Adam was given dominion on the sixth day. Not the authority he had earned. Authority God had conferred. The capacity to exercise genuine influence in the world — not from human sufficiency, but from the connection to the One who owns everything and moves through what is fully surrendered to Him.

That is what the next chapter describes.

Not confidence. Not a strategy. Not the accumulation of skill and influence through sufficient effort.

Empowerment.

XI

Empowerment: Living With Influence

"God has not given us a spirit of fear, but of power and love and self-control." — 2 Timothy 1:7

There is a difference between a life that is active and a life that has influence.

Activity is easy to produce. The calendar can be filled. The hours can be occupied. The visible markers of a full and productive life can be arranged and maintained. But activity and influence are not the same thing, and the person who has spent years confusing the two eventually discovers the difference in the most uncomfortable way — not through failure, but through the hollow quality of a fullness that has not actually moved anything.

Influence is not the same as impact in the conventional sense either. Impact can be manufactured at scale, by volume, or through the accumulation of visibility and reach. Influence is something more interior than that. It is what happens when a life organized around God's purposes becomes a conduit for something beyond the person's natural capacity. When the presence in the room shifts because of who is in it. When the conversation goes somewhere, it could not have gone without that particular person. When the outcome is not fully explained by the human resources assembled to produce it.

This is empowerment. Not a feeling of confidence, though it often produces that. Not the achievement of significant outcomes, though those sometimes follow. The lived experience of a life that is genuinely being carried by something larger than itself — that is operating not from the finite reserves of human capacity but from a connection to a source that does not deplete.

Hope restores the soul's ability to expect God. Abundance rebuilds the interior lens through which provision is received. Virtue produces character that holds across conditions. And empowerment is what becomes possible when the first three are genuinely present — when the soul that has been rebuilt around hope, organized around abundance, and expressed through consistent character becomes a life through which God's purposes can actually move.

The disciples' story is the most compressed and dramatic account available of what the difference between human capacity and divine empowerment actually looks like.

Three years. They had walked with Jesus across every kind of terrain and situation. They had watched Him heal, teach, confront, restore, and raise the dead. They had been sent out in pairs to minister in His name and had returned with accounts of what happened when they did. They had more proximity to the source of divine power than any group of people in human history.

And when the actual crisis arrived — the arrest in the garden, the trial, the crucifixion — they scattered. Peter denied knowing Him three times before dawn. They hid behind locked doors, afraid that what had happened to Jesus would happen to them next—the three years of proximity had not been sufficient to produce the kind of interior that could hold under that pressure.

This is not a story about their failure. It is a story about the limits of proximity without transformation. Knowledge about Jesus had not been adequate preparation for the moment. Having seen what He could do had not rebuilt the interior that would need to carry what they were called to carry. They had information and experience that far exceeded what most believers ever accumulate. They did not yet have the interior restructuring that would make what they knew available to them under pressure.

Then Pentecost. The same men, fifty days later, were unrecognizable. Peter — who had been unable to hold his claim to know Jesus under the questioning of a servant girl — stood in front of thousands of people in Jerusalem, in public, in daylight, before the same authorities who had crucified the One he was declaring, and spoke with a clarity and a weight that produced three thousand conversions in a single day.

Nothing external had changed. The authorities were still the authorities. The danger was still real. The social and political pressure to be quiet was still enormous. What had changed was entirely interior. Something had been placed in the interior that was not there before. Something that reorganized the governing center around a source that the threat of death could not reach. And from that reorganized interior, a life moved — not because Peter was trying harder or had summoned the courage that had failed him before. Because the interior from which he was now operating was built around something that a human threat could not reorganize.

Empowerment is not the achievement of confidence. It is the fruit of an interior rebuilt around a source that fear cannot reach.

The promise Jesus had given them before the crucifixion was specific: you will receive power when the Holy Spirit has come upon you, and you will be my witnesses in Jerusalem and in all Judea and Samaria, and to the end of the earth. The scope of that promise is worth sitting with. From the room where they were hiding to the end of the earth. From the men who could not hold their own in a courtyard conversation to the witnesses who would turn the Roman Empire inside out within a generation.

The power was not given to make their lives easier. It was not given to resolve their personal challenges or to guarantee favorable outcomes in their individual circumstances. It was given for a purpose that was larger than any of them, and that would require something no amount of human effort, training, or accumulated experience could produce. It was given so that the life, death, and resurrection of Jesus would reach people who had not heard, in languages the disciples had not learned, through situations the disciples had not anticipated, across generations the disciples would not live to see.

That kind of reach is not the product of human strategy, however well executed. It is the product of a divine intention moving through human vessels made available to carry it. The disciples became those vessels not by improving themselves to the point of adequacy but by being emptied of the self-reliance that had always been the limiting factor, and filled with a presence that had no such limit.

Paul's account of his own empowerment is more honest about the experience from the inside than the Acts narrative can be from the outside.

He had a thorn in the flesh. He does not tell us what it was, which may be deliberate — the lack of specificity allows every reader to bring their own version of the experience to the text. Something that was limiting him. Something he had prayed about three times, specifically asking for it to be removed, believing that without it, he would be more effective. And the answer he received was not yes.

My grace is sufficient for you, for my power is made perfect in weakness. This is a difficult answer to receive. It does not remove the limitation. It does not explain the limitation or provide a timeline for its resolution. It reframes the limitation entirely — presents it not as a deficit to be overcome before the real work can begin but as the precise condition in which God's power is most fully expressed. The weakness is not an obstacle to empowerment. In God's economy, it is the context for it.

Paul's response to this reframing is remarkable. He does not grit his teeth and accept the bad news. He says he will boast all the more gladly in his weaknesses, so that the power of Christ may rest upon him. The word translated as 'rest' carries the sense of taking up residence, settling in, and making a home. The weakness is not just the backdrop against which God's power is occasionally displayed. It is the space in which God's power lives.

This is not a theology of passivity or of embracing inadequacy as a spiritual virtue. Paul was the most relentlessly energetic minister in the New Testament record. He planned, wrote, argued, traveled, established, and fought for the integrity of the gospel with everything he had. He was not idle. But he had learned, through the thorn and the answer to the prayer about the thorn, that the energy he brought to the work was not the variable that determined its outcomes. What determined the outcomes was the power that moved through the work when the work was done in genuine dependence on the One who assigned it.

Therefore, I am content with weaknesses, insults, hardships, persecutions, and calamities. For when I am weak, then I am strong. The paradox is not wordplay. It is the honest description of what a life of genuine empowerment actually feels like from the inside. The strength is real. But it is not where strength is usually expected. It is located at the point of acknowledged inadequacy, where the human reserve has been genuinely exhausted, and what continues is not what the person produced.

The weakness is not an obstacle to empowerment. In God's economy, it is the context for it.

Moses is the Old Testament's clearest portrait of how empowerment moves through a person who has run completely out of reasons to believe they are adequate for what they are being asked to carry.

His objections to the burning bush were not performed in humility. They were accurate. He was not eloquent. He was not credible with the people he was being sent to lead. He had been out of Egypt for forty years and had spent most of that time tending sheep in a desert. By every reasonable measure, if you were assembling a team to confront the most powerful ruler in the world and demand the release of two million enslaved people, Moses was not the person you would draft first. Or tenth.

God's response to each objection was not to argue with Moses's self-assessment. He did not say Moses was more eloquent than he thought, or more credible, or more prepared. He said I will be with you. That is the entire answer. Not a list of Moses's overlooked strengths. Not a plan that worked around his limitations. Just the presence of the One who was sending him was the sufficient answer to every question about whether Moses was enough.

I will be with you. This is the foundational promise of empowerment in Scripture. Not that the person called is adequate. That the One who calls will be present with them as they go. The adequacy is in the accompaniment, not in the person being accompanied. And the person who has genuinely received this promise — not as a theological idea but as a governing conviction that shapes how they actually step into what they are called to do — is freed from the exhausting project of trying to be sufficient before they move.

Moses went. Haltingly, with Aaron alongside, still uncertain, still carrying the awareness of his own limitations into every confrontation with Pharaoh. But he went. And the plagues came not from Moses's authority but from the authority of the One behind him. And the sea parted not because Moses had finally generated enough faith to make it happen, but because the One who made the sea told it to move. And the two million people made it across, not because Moses had solved the logistics of moving that many people through the wilderness, but because manna appeared in the morning, water came from the rock, and the cloud led them where they needed to go.

The empowered life looks like this from the outside. Not a person who has assembled all the necessary resources before beginning. A person who has begun with what they have, in response to what they have been called to, trusting that what they do not have will be provided along the way. Not recklessness. Responsiveness. The willingness to move with what is available rather than waiting for the full inventory to be complete before taking the first step.

Gideon's story adds another dimension. Where Moses's limitation was public inadequacy — he was not the obvious candidate for a visible and demanding role — Gideon's limitation was internal. He was hiding when the angel found him. Threshing wheat in a wine press to conceal it from the Midianites, a picture of a person who has organized his life around avoiding the attention of the threat rather than addressing it.

The angel's greeting was almost ironic in its gap from observable reality. Mighty warrior. Gideon was hiding. He was the least in his family, from the weakest clan in Manasseh. He had a list of reasons why the mission being described to him could not possibly be assigned to him, and the list was not inaccurate.

What followed was one of the most methodical dismantlings of human self-sufficiency in the Old Testament. God reduced Gideon's army from thirty-two thousand to three hundred. Not because three hundred was logistically optimal. Because thirty-two thousand would have produced the wrong story. If 32,000 men routed the Midianite army, Israel would conclude it had won. Three hundred men, at night, with torches inside clay jars and rams' horns as their weapons, could only produce one conclusion: God did this.

The reduction was not a test of Gideon's faith. It was the construction of the conditions under which the outcome would be unambiguous. God was not interested in a victory that could be explained by human capacity. He was interested in a victory that would settle, for a generation, the question of who was governing Israel's story. And that kind of victory required the complete removal of the human capacity that would otherwise absorb the credit.

This is the logic of empowerment that runs consistently through Scripture. God does not typically work through people who have assembled sufficient resources before they begin. He works through people whose insufficiency is visible enough that what happens cannot be attributed to them. The three hundred. The five loaves and two fish. The walls of Jericho falling to trumpets and marching feet. The empty tomb. The story God keeps telling is a story in which human inadequacy is not the obstacle but the platform.

God does not typically work through people who have assembled sufficient resources before they begin. He works through people whose insufficiency is visible enough that what happens cannot be attributed to them.

Empowerment in the ordinary life of a believer is rarely as dramatic as any of these accounts. The burning bush does not typically appear. The army does not typically need to be reduced from 32,000 to 300. The visible miracle that makes the source of power unambiguous is not the normal texture of a Monday.

What empowerment looks like in the ordinary life is more subtle and in some ways more demanding, because the ordinary life does not produce the kind of obvious insufficiency that makes dependence on God the only available option. The ordinary life offers enough human competence, enough accumulated experience, enough natural intelligence and relational skill, to make it entirely possible to move through most of it without ever genuinely needing anything beyond what is already available.

The temptation of the empowered life in ordinary conditions is to operate from natural capacity. The default is to reserve the language of dependence on God for the moments when that capacity obviously fails. This is not dishonesty. It is the default of a soul that has not yet integrated the reality that natural capacity is itself a gift, that the intelligence and skill and relational wisdom being brought to the ordinary day are not self-generated any more than the miracle at Jericho was self-generated. They are what God has provided for this particular life and this particular calling. And they are meant to be used in the same posture of dependence that Moses brought to the burning bush — not because they are inadequate, but because the One who gave them is the One they are meant to serve.

The person whose interior has genuinely been reorganized around empowerment relates to their own capacity differently than the person who has not. They bring everything they have to the work — full effort, full intelligence, full preparation, full investment of what they have been given. And they hold the outcome in open hands. Not because they are indifferent to the outcome, but because they have learned, through enough experience, that the outcomes they most needed and did not produce themselves have tended to be better than the outcomes they planned and executed entirely on their own.

This holding of outcomes in open hands is not passivity. It is the active, deliberate, sometimes effortful posture of a person who is doing everything available to them and simultaneously trusting the results to a governance larger than their own. It is what Paul described as working out your salvation with fear and trembling — full effort, full seriousness, full engagement — while knowing that it is God who is at work in you, both to will and to work for his good pleasure. Both are true simultaneously. The work is real. The Source behind the work is real. And the person who is genuinely empowered holds both truths without collapsing one into the other.

The empowered life has a quality of forward motion that does not depend on favorable conditions. The person carrying fear as a governing orientation does not move until the conditions are sufficiently safe. They wait for the uncertainty to resolve, for the risk to become manageable, for the evidence that the next step will not be the one that costs them something they cannot afford to lose. And so they wait. And the conditions, which are never as safe as fear requires them to be, never quite become adequate. And the waiting becomes life.

The person whose interior has been rebuilt around empowerment does not require the conditions to be safe before moving. They require something different—the clarity of the call and the presence of the One who issued it. These two things together are sufficient for the next step, even when the next step is not fully visible, and the conditions are not yet favorable, and the outcome is genuinely uncertain.

This does not mean recklessness. Moses needed to be sent before he went. Gideon needed the confirmation of the fleece and the dream before he moved his three hundred men into the Midianite camp at night. Esther needed three days of fasting before she approached the king unsummoned. The empowered life is not characterized by impulsive action in response to every impulse that presents itself as divine leading. It is characterized by the willingness to move, with appropriate discernment, once the movement has been genuinely confirmed — without requiring the full safety that fear always demands and that faith never requires.

The person moving this way carries a quality of settled forward motion that is recognizable to the people around them. Not aggressiveness or a driven quality that overrides others' input. A steadiness. A willingness to be in motion toward what they are called to, even when the motion is costly, uncertain, or slow. A refusal to be permanently stopped by the obstacles that permanently stop people whose movement depends on the obstacles being removed first.

The empowered life does not require conditions to be
safe before moving. It requires the clarity of the call
and the presence of the One who issued it.

The influence that empowerment produces is not primarily about impressive output.

Output can be produced solely by effort. By sufficiently motivated human capacity, applied consistently over enough time, significant amounts of output can be generated. Books written, organizations built, relationships managed, platforms grown. All of this is possible without genuine empowerment, and much of it is produced that way every day.

The influence that empowerment produces is qualitatively different from what effort alone creates. It is the kind of influence that leaves something in a room long after the person has left it. That changes the direction of a conversation in a way that the conversation cannot quite account for. That produces in the people who receive it not merely the impression of competence or the impact of good content, but something that settles in the interior and continues working there.

This kind of influence is not the product of technique. The right communication strategy, presentation, or content cannot manufacture it. It is the overflow of an interior that is genuinely connected to a source that the technique cannot replicate. It is what happens when the person speaking is not primarily managing the impression they are making but is genuinely present to the people they are with and the God they are serving. It is the difference between a word that was well-crafted and a word that was genuinely given — and the people on the receiving end almost always know the difference, even when they cannot name it.

The disciples turned the world upside down, not because they were the most educated or the most strategically positioned or the most naturally gifted communicators of their generation. They turned it upside down because what came through them was not primarily them. And the people who encountered them encountered, in that encounter, something that their own natural experience of other human beings had not prepared them for.

This is the final fruit of the H.A.V.E. sequence. Not hope as a private interior experience, though it begins there. Not abundance as a personal orientation toward provision, though it is rooted there. Not virtue as a private achievement of character, though it is expressed there. All of it moving outward, through the empowered life, into the lives of the people God has placed in the path of that life. The alignment of the interior, through empowerment, becomes a source of alignment for others.

Not because the person set out to be influential. Because the One who empowers them has purposes that are larger than the person and that use the person, in the ordinary texture of their ordinary days, as the means by which those purposes reach the people they were always intended to reach.

This is empowerment. Not the destination, but the door through which everything that has been rebuilt in the interior becomes available to the world outside it. And it is available to every believer whose interior has been rebuilt to carry it.

Part Six: **The Sabbath Life**

XII

A Life That Holds Together

"So then you are no longer strangers and aliens, but you are fellow citizens with the saints and members of the household of God, built on the foundation of the apostles and prophets, Christ Jesus himself being the cornerstone, in whom the whole structure, being joined together, grows into a holy temple in the Lord." — Ephesians 2:19-21

On the seventh day, God rested.

Not because He was tired. Not because the work had depleted Him or because He needed recovery before He could continue. He rested because the work was finished. Because everything was functioning as it was designed to function. Because the architecture was intact, the sequence was ordered, and the created world was operating in the condition He had built it for. The rest was not the reward for sufficient effort. It was the natural atmosphere of a creation completed according to its design.

That is the picture of the life this chapter describes.

Not a life that has escaped difficulty. Not a life that has arrived at some permanent plateau beyond the reach of pressure and loss and the ordinary weight of ordinary days. A life whose interior has been rebuilt to the point where the operating mode is no longer striving. Where the governing posture is no longer management and effort, and the exhausting project of holding together what keeps wanting to fall apart. Where the soul has returned — not perfectly, not without ongoing formation, but genuinely — to the condition it was designed for.

Adam worked in the garden. The Sabbath did not eliminate work. It revealed the interior condition for which work was always meant to be done. Not toward rest. From it. The seventh day was not an interruption of the first six. It was their completion. The sign that everything was in its right place and operating as designed.

The life that holds together is the Sabbath life. Not a life of perpetual ease. A life whose governing center has been rebuilt to the point where the rest is no longer something to be achieved at the end of sufficient effort. It is the foundation from which every ordinary day is lived.

That is what the H.A.V.E. Effect produces. Not four qualities to maintain. The interior condition of a soul that has finally been returned to the design it was given on Day 6 — and can now live from Day 7.

There is a version of the Christian life that is perpetually under construction.

Not in the good sense — not the honest, ongoing formation of a person being shaped by God across the seasons of a life. In the anxious sense. The version in which the work of becoming is always one more discipline away from completion, one more breakthrough away from the stability that Sunday keeps promising, and Monday keeps dismantling, one more season of effort away from the coherent, integrated, recognizably aligned life that the believer has been reaching for since the beginning.

Most believers know this version. They have lived in it, some for years, some for decades. The gap between what is believed and what is experienced. The distance between the interior they carry into Sunday and the interior that remains by Friday. The quiet, persistent sense that the full life is adjacent to the life being lived — that it exists, that others seem to have found it, that it is somehow available, and that the reasons it has not arrived are located somewhere in the believer's own failure to do the right things consistently enough.

This book has argued something different.

The gap is not a discipline problem. It is a structural problem. The distance between Sunday and Monday is not created by insufficient effort applied to the right practices. It is created by an interior that has not yet been rebuilt around the right foundation. And the right foundation is not a set of practices. It is the Person in whom the whole structure is joined together and grows.

When the foundation is right, everything built on it holds differently. Not perfectly — the building is always in some state of ongoing formation. But it holds. The pressure of the ordinary week does not dismantle what was received on Sunday. The difficulty of the difficult season does not undo the clarity that came in the good one. Monday morning does not arrive as a return to what is real. It arrives as the next room in a house that is actually occupied.

The Hebrew word shalom is routinely translated as " peace, but the word carries a structural weight that peace does not fully convey in English.

Shalom means completeness. Wholeness. The condition of a thing that has all its parts and all its parts are in their right relationship to each other. When the Old Testament writers used shalom to describe the condition God intends for human beings, they were not describing the absence of conflict or the presence of pleasant circumstances. They were describing the condition of a life in which everything is where it is supposed to be — spirit governing soul, soul governing body, the whole person oriented toward God and thereby functioning as it was designed to function.

This is the life that holds together. Not the life that has been protected from difficulty. The life whose interior ordering is stable enough that difficulty does not reorganize it. The storm comes — and the life that has been built on the rock does not fall, because its foundation is not circumstances but the character and presence of the One who does not move when circumstances do.

Shalom is not achieved by removing the things that threaten it. It is built on a foundation that enables shalom even in their presence. The person whose interior has been genuinely rebuilt around the life of faith — whose hope has been restored, whose abundance lens has been recalibrated, whose character has been grown from a source that holds under pressure, whose empowerment flows from genuine connection to the Spirit rather than the management of personal capacity — that person carries shalom not as a circumstantial condition but as an interior architecture.

They are not undisturbed. They are not beyond the reach of grief or difficulty or the ordinary weight of a demanding life. But they are not reorganized by these things. The disturbance passes through a governing center that remains fixed. The grief is felt at its actual weight, neither amplified by anxiety nor suppressed by the performance of faith. The difficulty is navigated by a soul that has somewhere to stand while the navigation is happening.

That somewhere is not a technique or a set of practices, though practices matter. It is a Person. The cornerstone, as Paul described Him, is the fixed point in whom the whole structure is joined together, from whom the whole structure derives its coherence, without whom the parts are simply parts rather than a building.

Shalom is not the absence of difficulty. It is the presence of a foundation that makes the difficulty impossible to reach.

Paul's letter to the Colossians contains a phrase that has become so familiar that it is easy to read past it.

"As you received Christ Jesus the Lord, so walk in him, rooted and built up in him and established in the faith."

Three verbs. Rooted. Built up. Established. Each one describes a different dimension of what the life that holds together actually looks like in practice.

Rooted. The image is agricultural — a plant whose root system goes deep enough and wide enough that it cannot be toppled by ordinary weather. The depth of the root determines the stability of what grows above ground. A shallow-rooted plant may look identical to a deep-rooted one in favorable conditions. The difference only becomes visible when the conditions change — when the wind comes, when the drought arrives, when the pressure that reveals what is actually holding the plant up is applied.

The believer who is rooted in Christ is not distinguished from the believer who is not by the quality of their spiritual expression in favorable conditions. Both may worship with genuine feeling, serve with genuine effort, and speak about God with genuine conviction when Sunday is good and the week has been kind. The distinction becomes visible when the conditions change, when the diagnosis arrives. When the relationship fractures. When the project fails. When Monday morning is the eighteenth in a row that has felt like the same returning weight, the rooted believer is not undamaged by any of this. But they are not uprooted. The root goes to a source that the weather cannot reach.

Built up. The image shifts from agriculture to architecture. A structure that is being added to — not completed in a single moment but growing, over time, into something more substantial than what it was at the beginning. The life of faith is not a destination reached but a building under construction. Each season adds something. Each difficulty shapes something. Each act of faithfulness, however small, becomes part of the structure. And the structure, over time, accumulates a weight and a presence that is different from what could have been assembled quickly.

This is why the life that holds together is not typically young. Not in years necessarily — some people are built up remarkably quickly because the seasons they walk through are remarkably formative. But in depth. The person who has been rooted and built up over time carries something that the person who has only recently been rooted cannot yet carry. Not superiority. Weight. The accumulated weight of a life that has been through things and has not been dismantled by them and has continued to be built up on the other side of them.

Established. The third image is more abstract but no less structural. To be established is to be settled at the level of the governing convictions that determine how everything else is processed. The established person is not easily destabilized by new arguments against what they believe, because what they believe is not primarily held as an argument. It is held as a lived reality, tested in actual conditions, confirmed by experience, and integrated into the actual texture of how they move through the world. You cannot argue a person out of what they have genuinely lived.

Rooted. Built up. Established. These are not descriptions of spiritual achievement. They are descriptions of what a life looks like when it has been genuinely given to the right foundation.

The life that holds together is recognizable in the ordinary day in ways that have nothing to do with spectacular spiritual experience.

It is recognizable in the quality of the Monday morning. Not that Monday is easy or that the weight of the week is absent. But the person who woke up on Sunday is still present on Monday. The connection between the clarity received in worship and the capacity available in the ordinary day is not severed by the transition. The revelation does not require reconstruction. The interior that carried it into Sunday is the same one that carries it into Monday, because the governing center has not changed; only the context has.

This is the Sunday/Monday Gap closing. Not the gap between Sunday feeling and Monday feeling — feelings will continue to vary with circumstances, with sleep, with the particular demands of the particular week. The gap between Sunday identity and Monday identity. Between who the person is before God and who the person is at the desk, in the meeting, in the difficult conversation, in the moment when no one is watching, and the shortcut is available, and the cost of integrity is real.

When that gap closes — not perfectly, not without ongoing formation, but genuinely — the life that results is not more religious in the conventional sense. It is a more coherent life. A life in which the parts fit together because they are all organized around the same foundation. The prayer room and the boardroom are not different theaters requiring different performances. They are different rooms in the same house, inhabited by the same person, ordered by the same governing center.

This coherence is what others notice first, though they often cannot name it. They notice that the person is the same in different contexts. That's what they say about their faith on Sunday, but are not embarrassed by how they behave on Monday. The quality of their presence in difficulty is not dramatically different from that in ease. That they seem to have somewhere to stand that is not determined by what is happening around them.

This is not a performance of stability. The person who has genuinely arrived here is not working to appear a certain way. They are a certain way, because the interior has been rebuilt around a foundation that the ordinary fluctuations of life cannot fundamentally reorganize.

The generosity of the life that holds together is one of its most quietly striking features.

Not generosity as a discipline imposed on an otherwise tight-fisted soul. The natural, largely unrehearsed generosity of a person whose interior is organized around abundance rather than scarcity — who holds what they have in open hands because the governing conviction about provision has been genuinely rebuilt, not just intellectually affirmed.

This generosity extends well beyond money, though it includes money. It is generosity of attention — the capacity to be actually present to the person in front of them, rather than managing how the interaction is going or calculating what it costs. Generosity of time — the willingness to be interrupted, to invest in something that will not yield a visible return, to give the hour that the relationship requires rather than the hour the schedule allocated. Generosity of credit — the ease with which a person whose identity is not organized around recognition can acknowledge the contribution of others without the diminishment that acknowledgment costs someone who is keeping score.

All of this flows from the same source. The soul that has been rebuilt around God's provision does not experience the giving of what it has as a threat to what remains. It has learned — through enough experience, through enough seasons of releasing and finding that the source replenishes what was released — that the open hand is not the vulnerable hand. It is the hand through which the most continues to flow.

The gratitude of this life is similarly unrehearsed. Not the performed gratitude of someone who has been told that grateful people are happier and is applying the practice accordingly. The genuine, sometimes slightly surprised gratitude of a person who has learned to receive what is actually present rather than filtering it through the lens of what is still absent. Who can sit in an ordinary Tuesday — nothing remarkable happening, no visible confirmation of God's faithfulness arriving that day — and find, in the ordinary Tuesday, genuine evidence of a God who is present and providing and worth thanking.

The life that holds together is not the life that has been given everything. It is the life that can receive what it has been given.

The relationships that hold a life together have a particular quality that is different from both the relational performance of the person managing impressions and the relational exhaustion of the person who is giving from a depleted reserve.

They are present. Genuinely, unhurriedly, without the quality of managed engagement that people can feel even when they cannot name it. The person in front of them is actually being seen rather than efficiently processed. The conversation they are in is actually being attended to rather than monitored for how it is going and what impression it is making.

This quality of presence is one of the rarest things in ordinary human interaction, and people are often profoundly affected by encountering it without being able to say precisely what it is. They felt heard. They felt seen. They felt that what they brought to the conversation actually mattered, rather than being received, sorted, and filed. This is the fruit of an interior that is not preoccupied with itself — that has enough of its governing concerns settled that it has genuine attention available to give to the person in front of it.

They are also honest in a way that is neither unkind nor brutal. The person whose identity is not organized around being liked does not need to say what will be well received rather than what is true. They can tell the truth in love — not as a theological accomplishment requiring conscious effort, but as the natural expression of a soul that cares genuinely about the other person and is not simultaneously managing the impression their honesty will make. The truth arrives with warmth because the warmth is real, not because it has been added as a softening technique.

They love without the transaction. This is perhaps the most distinctive relational feature of the life that holds together — the absence of the implicit ledger that most relational engagement maintains. No running account of what has been given and what has been returned. No adjustment of investment based on how the investment has been valued. No gradual withdrawal when the relationship costs more than it returns. Love offered as a gift rather than an exchange, because the soul offering it is not operating from a reserve that needs to be protected.
None of this means the person has no limits, no needs, or is available for every demand placed on them. The life that holds together is not the life that has dissolved into availability. It is the life that gives from genuine

surplus rather than managed deficit, that sets limits from clarity rather than from fear, that is present in the relationships where it is called to be present and absent from the ones where presence would be something other than love.

The work of life that holds together is done differently from the work of the person whose identity depends on how the work goes.

Full effort. That does not change. The person of genuine faith is not less industrious or less excellent in their professional engagement because their identity is not organized around the outcomes. Often, it is because the energy previously consumed by background anxiety about self-protection has been freed for the actual work. The soul that is not managing its own reputation has all of its capacity available for the task.

But the outcomes are held in open hands. The stalled project is not a verdict on the person's worth. The season in which the work produces nothing visible is not evidence of divine abandonment. The recognition that goes to someone else is not a signal that the person's contribution has gone unnoticed by the only One whose noticing ultimately determines anything. The soul whose identity is rooted in something that work outcomes cannot reach is free to do the work without the weight of needing the work to return something that only God can actually give.

This produces a quality of workplace steadiness that is recognizable and rare. Not the steadiness of someone who does not care — the person cares deeply. The steadiness of someone whose caring is not organized around fear. Who can receive the disruption, the redirect, the failed launch, the difficult colleague, the unreasonable deadline, with the full engagement of a person who is actually present to the situation and the genuine equanimity of a person whose center is not located in the situation's outcome.

The work becomes an act of worship in the most literal sense — not in the sense of being performed with religious intensity, but in the sense of being offered. Whatever you do, work heartily, as for the Lord and not for men. The work done this way is not the work of a person trying to be spiritual in the workplace. It is the work of a person for whom the workplace and the prayer room are both rooms in the same house, both offered to the same Lord, both expressions of the same governing orientation.

When the workplace and the prayer room are in the same house, the work becomes an act of offering rather than a performance.

The life that holds together does not mean a life without struggle.

This is important to say clearly, because the alternative reading — that alignment produces a life in which difficulty is largely absent, in which the hard things resolve quickly, in which the peace is felt consistently, and the clarity is always available — is a misreading of both Scripture and experience. The most aligned lives in Scripture are among the most costly. Abraham's life of faith included years of waiting for what had been promised, the terrible test of the mountain, the ordinary grief of aging and loss. David's life included Psalm 22 as surely as Psalm 23. Paul's life included the thorn alongside the visions. Jeremiah's life of faithfulness included decades of apparent fruitlessness alongside the words that have shaped believers for three thousand years.

The aligned life is not protected from difficulty. It is equipped to carry difficulty differently. The grief is still grief. The uncertainty is still uncertain. The long seasons of waiting are still long. But they are carried by an interior that has somewhere to stand, that has a governing center that the difficulty cannot permanently displace, that has a cord running to a fixed point that the storm cannot cut.

And across time — which is the frame in which the aligned life is most honestly evaluated — the pattern becomes visible. Not that every difficulty was resolved as hoped. That the person came through. That which was built did not fall. That the foundation held when the floods came, and the wind blew, and the streams beat against the house. That at the end of the season, or the year, or the decade, what remains standing is recognizably the same person who entered it — not unchanged, not undamaged, but not unmade. Still rooted, still built up, still established in the faith that has been tested and found reliable.

This is the testimony that the aligned life produces over time. Not the testimony of a spectacular moment. The testimony of a consistent posture across the ordinary accumulation of days, weeks, seasons, and years. The testimony that faith actually works — not in the sense of producing comfortable outcomes, but in the sense of producing a life that actually holds together.

A life that can be given to others. That has something to offer the people who are still in the gap, who are still living the Sunday/Monday separation, who have not yet found the foundation that makes a coherent life possible. A life that, simply by being what it is, points toward what alignment with God actually produces in a human being who has genuinely allowed it.

The aligned life is not protected from difficulty. It is equipped to carry difficulty differently.

We began this book with a simple observation: that most believers do not struggle because they lack faith. They struggle because their lives are structurally misaligned with their beliefs.

The gap between Sunday and Monday is not a character flaw. It is not evidence of insufficient devotion or inadequate effort or a permanent condition of spiritual second-tier membership. It is a structural problem with a structural answer. The interior that cannot carry Sunday's clarity into Monday's demands is not broken. It is an unbuilt one. And the God who began a good work in the believer is fully capable of completing it — not through the accumulation of more religious activity, but through the genuine, progressive, sometimes painful, ultimately reliable rebuilding of the interior around the foundation that can actually hold.

Hope arrives first. Quiet, structural, the first evidence that something has shifted at the level of the governing center. The cord is becoming taut again. The soul's expectation of God begins to recalibrate around who He actually is, rather than who fear has made Him out to be.

Abundance follows. The lens through which provision is received is beginning to clear. The scarcity filter is losing its governing authority.

The open hand is becoming more natural than the closed one. The soul begins to receive what has been there all along, now that the framework through which it arrives has been rebuilt.

Virtue takes shape. Character that holds across conditions. The gap between the person presented and the person who is actually there is beginning to narrow. The exhausting work of self-management gives way to the simpler, more durable expression of a soul that is becoming genuinely integrated. Tamim — the same on every surface.

And empowerment. The life that has been rebuilt from the inside out becomes a life through which God's purposes actually move. The natural capacity is still present and fully engaged, and through it and beyond it, something that the natural capacity cannot account for. Ordinary life becomes a conduit for influence that exceeds what the person could have produced from what they had.

This is the H.A.V.E. Effect. Not a formula. A description. The honest account of what God produces in a life that has been genuinely returned to Him — not as a religious performance but as a structural surrender, the interior rebuilt around the foundation it was always designed for.

I want to take you back to a parking lot.

Two years ago, overdrawn. The weight of everything that wasn't working pressed in from every direction. The quiet accumulation of months of wrestling with failure and inadequacy, and the growing suspicion that something fundamental had gone wrong. A man sitting in a car who had been teaching about the abundant life to other people, while privately unable to find the door to it himself.

And then a whisper.

"You already have what you need."

I have spent the years since that afternoon trying to understand what that whisper meant—trying to trace it back to its source. Trying to build a framework that could hold what it was saying clearly enough that other people — people in their own versions of the parking lot, carrying their own versions of the weight — could hear it too.

This book is what I found.

The provision was always present. The problem was not absence. It was misalignment. What I was experiencing in that parking lot was not a man who had been given too little. It was a man whose interior had not yet been rebuilt to receive what had already been given. The gap between who I was on Sunday and who I was on Monday was not evidence of insufficient faith, inadequate effort, or some permanent condition of spiritual deficiency. It was the structurally inevitable result of an interior that had not yet been restored to the order for which it was designed.

And the whisper — you already have what you need — was pointing somewhere more precise than I understood in the moment.

It was pointing to Day 6.

To the morning before the first Monday existed. To the moment when God looked at the human being He had just made and blessed him — not after he had worked for it, not after he had proven worthy of it, not after he had demonstrated the kind of consistency that would justify the investment. Before any of that. Before the first day of work. Before the first test. Before the first failure.

The cord. The lens. The integrated life. The conferred authority. Hope and abundance and virtue and empowerment — all of it placed in human hands on a morning when no Monday had yet arrived to test whether it would hold.

You already have what you need.

Not as a consolation. As a theological fact. The inheritance was given before the fall took it. The design was built before the disorder reversed it. The foundation exists before you begin building on it. And the God who gave it on Day 6 is the same God who is working, right now, to restore what disorder broke — to bring the human soul back into the condition it was always meant to inhabit, so that the person who shows up on Sunday and the person who shows up on Monday are finally, durably, the same person.

The gap can close.

Not all at once. Not without cost. Not without the ongoing, lifelong process of formation that is simply the shape of a faith that is alive. But genuinely, structurally, in ways that are felt on Monday morning and visible across the ordinary week and recognizable over the accumulation of seasons. The interiors of Sunday and Monday are converging. The life believed to begin is the life actually lived.

That is the H.A.V.E. Effect.

That is a life that holds together.

And it is available to every person willing to let the rebuilding begin.

The gap has a name.

And so does what replaces it.

Hope. Abundance. Virtue. Empowerment.

Not as goals to be achieved.

As the inheritance, you are returning to.

Throughout this book, I have used the names most familiar to the reader — God, the Lord, Jesus — so the message reaches as many people as possible without unnecessary barriers. But I want to honor Him here by name. And I want to be honest about why.

My study of Scripture has led me to a deep conviction that the Creator of the universe carries a personal name — Yahuah — and that His Son's name is Yahusha. This is not a peripheral theological opinion. It is woven into the fabric of Scripture itself. In Exodus 3:15, when Moses asked God who he should say sent him, the answer was direct and permanent: *"This is my name forever, and thus I am to be remembered throughout all generations."* The Psalms carry the same weight — Psalm 91:14 records His own words: *"I will protect him, because he knows my name."* Doesn't know about me. Knows my name. In Proverbs 18:10, the writer declares: *"The name of Yahuah is a strong tower; the righteous man runs into it and is safe."* And Yahusha himself made the connection unmistakably clear in John 5:43: *"I have come in my Father's name."* The Son carried the Father's name. Yahusha — Yah saves. The name of the Father is embedded in the name of the Son. This was not a coincidence. It was a declaration. And in John 17:6, Yahusha confirmed that revealing the Father's name was central to his entire mission on earth: *"I have manifested your name to the people whom you gave me out of the world."*

The name was never meant to be hidden. It was meant to be known, called upon, and carried.

This has not been merely an academic discovery for me. It has been a deeply personal one. Since coming to understand His name and to call upon Him by it, I have felt Him answer in ways I had not experienced before. The distance I sometimes felt in prayer began to close. The relationship became more intimate, more alive — as if something in the calling out of His name created a nearness I had been reaching for without knowing exactly what I was reaching toward. There is a difference between speaking to a title and speaking to a Person. When I began calling Him Yahuah, I encountered Him in a different way. Not as a concept. Not as a theological category. As the living God who said His name was to be remembered forever — and who keeps His word.

I recognize this may be new territory for some readers. I am not writing this to divide or to make the message harder to receive. I am writing it because honesty requires it. The H.A.V.E. Effect is a book about alignment — about closing the gap between what we believe and how we live. It would be a contradiction to write a book about that kind of integrity while withholding the most personal conviction I carry about the God the book is written for.

The sacred names are not a wall between this message and the people it was written for. They are a door — and I leave it open for every reader who feels the pull to walk through it.

To Yahuah be the glory.

James E. Nance II is the founder of the Sunday/Monday Gap™ — a faith-based coaching framework that helps believers close the gap between their Sunday clarity and their Monday reality. Armed with a bachelor's in economics and trained through Lipscomb University's ICF Level 2 accredited Performance Coaching program — one of the most rigorous coach training designations in the country — James brings both analytical precision and proven coaching methodology to the alignment problem most believers can't name.

Two years ago, James was sitting in a parking lot, overdrawn, coaching people toward alignment while quietly living outside of it himself. That moment became the turning point that gave birth to The H.A.V.E. Effect — not as a theory, but as a framework he has been living toward, returning to, and being rebuilt by ever since.

Through the D-Zone diagnostic, one-on-one coaching, and the Gap Activation Sprint™, James has helped hundreds of believers identify exactly where the gap lives in their lives — and what it takes to close it for good.
James lives with his wife and children in Oklahoma.

To Book James for Speaking

James is available for keynote addresses, church engagements, leadership conferences, and corporate events centered on the Sunday/Monday Gap framework.

To inquire about booking, email **james@jamesenance.com**

Ready to find out where your gap lives?
Take the D-Zone Assessment at
sundaymondaygap.com
Five minutes. A precise diagnosis. The interior work starts here.